500

fish & seafood dishes

500

fish & seafood dishes

Judith Fertig

APPLE

A Quintet Book

First published in the UK in 2011 by
Apple Press
7 Greenland Street
London NW1 0ND
United Kingdom

www.apple-press.com

ISBN: 978-1-84543-380-2
QTT.FSD

This book was conceived, designed, and produced by
Quintet Publishing Limited
6 Blundell Street
London N7 9BH
United Kingdom

Food Stylist: Valentina Sforza
Photographer: Ian Garlick
Designer: Rod Teasdale
Art Director: Michael Charles
Editorial Assistants: Carly Beckerman-Boys, Holly Willsher
Managing Editor: Donna Gregory
Publisher: James Tavendale

10 9 8 7 6 5 4 3 2 1

Printed in China by 1010 Printing International Ltd.

contents

introduction

If there is one food that most people hesitate to add to their culinary repertoire, it's probably seafood. But it's really a very simple food to prepare, and you'll get loads of compliments every time you do it.

This book helps demystify preparing and cooking seafood. Whether you wish to eat your seafood as is – oysters on the half shell, gravlax, sushi or crudo, for example – or you prefer to cook it in any number of ways, this book has a recipe and a technique for you.

Long ago, the only fish or shellfish available to cooks was the locally caught variety or preserved seafood, such as salted and dried cod in European cuisine, smoked fish in Africa or dried prawns in Chinese culture. The problem was transportation. Fish and shellfish are very perishable and can go from delicate and briny to mushy with the 'off' aroma of ammonia in a day or so.

Today, seafood is shipped, iced-down, from coast to coast on the same day it's caught. You can also buy 'FAS' fish and shellfish that have been 'frozen at sea' the same day they're caught. Freshwater catfish or farmed prawns can be 'IQF' or 'individually quick frozen'. Catfish farmers in the Mississippi Delta can net a catfish pond and transport the fish in a tank lorry to the processing plant nearby, where the fish go from whole fish to frozen fillets in a matter of hours.

what is fresh?

So, what is fresh? Freshness is apparent in the smell, texture and taste, not always in the state in which seafood is offered for sale.

In a blind taste test from the Chef's Collaborative, a group of culinary professionals sampled simply prepared fish and shellfish – some of it 'fresh' and never frozen, some of it frozen at sea. Sometimes, the frozen-at-sea product was better. If you recall the film *The Perfect Storm*, you remember that they had been fishing for days and had iced down the swordfish. If they had returned to port safely, the swordfish would have been several days old already. Is that fresh?

To further complicate matters, fish that is offered for sale 'fresh' at many fishmongers or supermarkets has actually been thawed from frozen.

Whether the seafood you're buying is fresh or thawed from frozen, the best way to determine freshness is with your eyes and nose, so go to a quality fishmonger – don't buy fish at a supermarket unless you are absolutely certain they have top-quality fish. Don't be afraid to ask the fishmonger if you can smell or touch the fish before you buy.

* Whole fish should have clear eyes and a briny, fresh aroma.
* Clams, mussels and oysters should have tightly closed shells and a briny aroma.
* Fish fillets and steaks should be delicate yet firm and have a sweet, briny aroma.

* Squid, calamari and octopus should be firm to the touch and have a sweet, briny aroma.
* Scallops out of the shell as well as prawns should be firm to the touch and have a sweet, briny aroma.
* Crabs, crayfish, langoustines and lobsters should be alive and moving, or cooked, with their meat picked out of the shell and chilled, tinned or frozen.

seafood substitution chart

Use this guide to help you select the freshest fish and shellfish at the fishmonger. If your seafood choice is not available, substitute another fish/shellfish from the same category. Also, if a fish is endangered, substitute one that is abundant.

	mild flavour	moderate flavour	full flavour
firm texture	lobster monkfish sea bass softshell crab prawns halibut	john dory salmon shark skate sturgeon swordfish cobia	cuttlefish escolar ono marlin squid tuna oysters
medium-firm texture	catfish grouper haddock halibut ocean perch pompano scallops snapper striped bass tilefish whitefish wolffish	arctic char barracuda mahi mahi porgy trout salmon fillet tilapia walleye pike	amberjack mullet kingfish mackerel permit sablefish yellowtail jack yellowtail snapper wahoo
delicate texture	bass (freshwater) cod flounder fluke hake pink snapper red snapper sand dab turbot	butterfish herring pomfret shad smelt/whitebait	anchovies bluefish buffalofish sardines

equipment

Seafood can be prepared with the usual indoor kitchen equipment: blender or food processor, chopping board and knives, kitchen scales, pots and pans, garlic press, grater, wooden spoons, etc. Outdoors, a simple barbecue with a lid and barbecue equipment such as tongs and spatula are enough to get you started. But if you want to take a very authentic approach to global seafood cuisine, you might want to check out the following kitchen helpers.

deep-fryer
With a deep-fryer, you can set the temperature, heat the oil and fry seafood in an exact yet effortless way.

barbecue wok
This metal wok, with perforations to let the barbecue flavours reach the food, allows you to stir-barbecue seafood, turning the food with wooden paddles or long-handled, metal barbecue spatulas.

hardwood chips
Bags of hardwood chips – apple, or if available, mesquite, hickory, etc. – are available at hardware shops or supermarkets in the barbecue section. Use a handful to give your seafood a slightly smoky flavour.

hardwood planks

Thin barbecuing or thick oven planks made from cedar, alder, maple or oak are used to plank-cook seafood on the barbecue or in the oven.

oyster knife

With heavy gloves and a sturdy, wide-bladed oyster knife, you can learn to open the most uncooperative oyster.

oventop smoker

This metal pan with a lid and a handle allows you to smoke foods indoors on your hob. You place a small amount of very fine wood chips in the centre of the bottom, cover with the tray, place the food on a rack on the tray, then close the lid to smoke. Small foods like fish fillets or prawns can be smoked in minutes this way.

sushi mat

The sushi mat is a simple woven bamboo rectangle. You layer your sushi ingredients on the mat, then use its sturdiness to help you roll the delicate ingredients together.

thermometer

A cooking thermometer, clipped to the side of a pan of oil, will let you know the temperature of the oil so seafood fries up crisp and golden.

seafood preparation tips

There are a variety of ways to prepare seafood, but there are a few basic guidelines to follow, whatever method you use:

* For food safety reasons, keep fish and shellfish – especially shellfish – chilled until you're ready to serve raw or cook.

* When in doubt, go for underdone. Fish and shellfish continue to cook for a minute or so more, away from the heat, and that can make a big difference, so pull them off the heat a minute or so before you're sure they're done. Worst case scenario? The seafood is a bit undercooked, and you can put it back in the poacher, in the oven, or under the grill to get it more done if necessary. But once it's overcooked, there's nothing you can do.

* Understand which is the skin side and the flesh side on fish fillets. Even when the skin has been removed from a fish fillet, you can still see darkened areas where it used to be. So when you follow the directions for barbecuing or planking fish, you'll know which side is which.

frying

Fish fillets and shellfish take best to frying. Fish steaks tend to curl up and whole fish do best deep-fried, but they require a big pan and a lot of oil. Thinner fillets like sole can be sautéed, while thicker fillets such as cod taste great with a batter and deep-fried.

Rinse and pat dry the seafood before adding any batter or coating. Make sure the oil is hot – about 190°C (375°F) – before you start frying. Do a test run with a small piece of bread if you're not sure. If the bread starts to sizzle and bubble around the edges as soon as it hits the oil, you're ready. You can also invest in a cooking thermometer or use a temperature-controlled deep fryer to gauge the temperature of the oil. Seafood is done when it is golden brown on all sides. Larger pieces of fish or shellfish will need to be turned as soon as one side is golden brown. When the seafood is done, remove it with a slotted spoon or pancake turner to drain on paper towels.

Barbecuing fish fillets – the more delicate flesh-side down first, then flipping over to the sturdier skin-side – helps the fillets stay together better. Only turn them once, using a wide-bladed fish spatula.

A high heat is actually better for barbecuing fish, as the surface gets crusty fast and makes fillets easier to turn with the help of a fish spatula – one with a wider metal spatula end.

barbecuing

A high heat, some oil or melted butter and the seasoning or marinade of your choice are all you need to barbecue perfect fish and shellfish. The high heat makes the surface get crusty quickly (with fillets, start with the delicate flesh-side down first, which helps the fillet stay together), and then you flip the fish over – just once – with a wide-bladed fish spatula. The fat, such as olive oil or melted butter, helps keep seafood from drying out during barbecuing and keeps it from sticking to the grill. The marinade imbues seafood with flavour – but just be careful not to marinate fish or shellfish for more than 30 minutes in an acidic marinade or you could end up with ceviche – delicious, but not what you were intending when you fired up the barbecue.

Barbecue most fish fillets over a high heat for 10 minutes per $2\frac{1}{2}$ cm of thickness – measure the thickness in the thickest part of the fillet before you barbecue. Fillets are generally 2 cm thick, so the total barbecuing time would be $7\frac{1}{2}$ minutes or about 3–4 minutes per side. The exception is meaty fish such as tuna, swordfish and shark, which many people like to eat rare to medium. These types of fish will be well-done over a high heat in 6–7 minutes per $2\frac{1}{2}$ cm of thickness. They tend to overcook and dry out more quickly than other fish. If you want a rare tuna steak, barbecue it for 1–2 minutes per side over a high heat.

If you think your fish is very delicate, use a perforated barbecue rack, and oil both the fish and the rack before you cook. If you're a novice and worried about your skills, start out with inexpensive, medium-textured, farm-raised cod for practice.

oven-baking & roasting

You can bake almost any type of fish and shellfish, from fish fillets and steaks to whole fish, to shellfish of all kinds. Generally, baking is done at a temperature around 175°C (350°F/Gas mark 4) until the seafood is lightly browned and done. A relatively short baking time and buttery moisture keeps fish and shellfish tender and succulent in the oven.

Roasting, usually done at temperatures above 200°C (400°F/Gas mark 6), works best with prawn, oysters, whole fish and thicker fish fillets. Fish steaks tend to curl up when roasted, and thin fish fillets are better grilled, planked, baked or sautéed. As you would for grilling, brush seafood with a fat such as olive oil or butter or a sauce to help keep it from drying out for the brief time it's in the oven.

planking

Planking is the simplest way to cook on the grill – just place the seafood on a plank on the grill and close the lid. With planked seafood, you get the gentle, aromatic flavour of the wood quite different from the flavour of grilling or smoking. You prepare an indirect fire, with the heat on one side and no heat on the other. The plank goes on the side with no heat. Basically, there are two types of hardwood planks that work well on the grill. Flat, thin planks (usually sold in packages) are for cooking foods without drizzly sauces that might drip and cause flare-ups on the grill. Thicker cedar oven planks with a well in the centre can also be used on the grill and work well for seafood dishes with lots of butter or sauces. Make sure you soak the plank (thick or thin) in cold water for at least 30 minutes before putting it on the barbecue.

poaching, steaming & simmering

Water that is gently simmering is kinder to delicate fish and shellfish and results in better texture than boiling water, which makes seafood more rubbery. When making a seafood soup or stew, you generally start by building flavour in the broth, adding and cooking vegetables under tender, then adding the fish and shellfish towards the end of cooking so that they don't cook any longer than necessary.

serving fish raw

Raw fish should be as fresh as possible. 'Sashimi grade' is the highest-quality raw fish you can buy, so go for that grade when you want to serve it. To cut fish into really thin slices for crudo or sushi, freeze a whole piece of fish for 30 minutes or so, then slice with a sharp knife. Keep all raw fish or shellfish chilled until ready to serve.

smoking

There are two ways to smoke fish and shellfish. Cold smoking preserves seafood, but doesn't cook it; cold smoking requires special equipment. Hot smoking cooks seafood, but doesn't preserve it; you can hot-smoke on your barbecue or in a oventop smoker. The recipes in this book are for hot smoking. To hot-smoke seafood, you need to prepare an indirect fire in your barbecue. This means the fire is on one side of the barbecue only. Then add wood to the fire so that it smolders and smokes. For a charcoal barbecue, add hardwood chips to the hot coals. For a gas barbecue, place them in a metal smoker box or an aluminium foil packet with holes poked in it, and set it close to a flame. To cook, place your seafood on the no-heat side of the barbecue. When you see the first wisp of smoke, close the barbecue to smoke your food.

raw bar

Every culture has its own delicious way to enjoy

uncooked seafood – gravlax in Scandinavia, sushi in

Japan, ceviche in Peru, crudo in Italy. Served on a

chilled plate or in a cocktail glass, raw fish looks and

tastes wonderful garnished with herbs, spices or a

drizzle of sauce.

oysters on the half shell

see variations page 38

From Belon (France) to Blue Point (New England), Sydney Rock (Australia and New Zealand), or Kumamoto (California), oyster varieties differ in size, brininess and flavour depending on their oceanic region. Have your fishmonger open the oysters for you or wear heavy gloves and use an oyster knife to pry the molluscs apart – right before serving. Dip each oyster into your favourite sauce or simply enjoy with a squeeze of fresh lemon.

for the mignonette sauce
225 ml (8 fl oz) dry white wine
100 ml (4 fl oz) red wine vinegar
50 g (2 oz) minced shallots
1½ tsp black peppercorns, crushed
⅛ tsp salt

rock salt
2 dozen fresh oysters on the half shell
fresh lemon wedges, to garnish

Whisk the wine and wine vinegar together in a small saucepan and bring to the boil. Cook until reduced to 175 ml (6 fl oz) (about 5 minutes). Stir in shallots, peppercorns and salt.

Chill for 2 hours.

Cover a platter with rock salt, 2½ cm deep. Arrange the chilled oysters on the rock salt and garnish with lemon wedges. Portion sauce into 4 dipping sauce bowls. Serve immediately.

Serves 4

fresh tuna carpaccio

see variations page 39

Thin slices of raw tuna, drizzled with a zesty sauce, make for a colourful and pleasing appetiser platter. Based on a raw beef dish named after the fifteenth-century artist Vittore Carpaccio and served at Harry's Bar in Venice, tuna carpaccio looks as good as it tastes. Sashimi-grade indicates the freshest, best-quality fish meant to be eaten raw.

225–450 g (½–1 lb) sashimi-grade tuna, cut
   2½ cm (1 in) thick, skin removed, rinsed
   and patted dry
175 g (6 oz) good-quality mayonnaise
1 tbsp grainy mustard

2 tbsp fresh lemon juice
extra-virgin olive oil
1 tbsp capers, drained, to garnish
coarse sea salt, to taste

Wrap and chill the tuna in the freezer for an hour or two, until it is stiff but not frozen through. Slice it horizontally into four ½-cm- (¼-in-) thick pieces. Put a slice of tuna between two pieces of waxed paper and pound gently from the centre outwards, until about ⅓ cm (⅛ in) thick. Repeat with the other slices. Place the slices, still in the waxed paper, in the refrigerator until ready to serve.

Whisk the mayonnaise, mustard and lemon juice together in a bowl until smooth. Spoon into a sealable plastic bag. To serve, drizzle the olive oil on a platter and top with the tuna pieces. Snip a bottom corner of the plastic bag and squeeze a pattern of carpaccio sauce over the tuna. Garnish with capers and a sprinkle of salt.

Serves 4

asian raw fish salad

see variations page 40

Known in China as yu sheng or yee sheng, and translated as 'rainbow raw fish salad' this dish has a wonderful variety of colours, tastes and textures. Use the method for cutting thin slices of tuna carpaccio, then vary the other ingredients by season or preference.

for the marinade
225 g (8 oz) tuna or
    yellowtail, thinly sliced
    (see method on page 24),
    rinsed and patted dry
1 (2½-cm/1-in) piece fresh
    root ginger, shredded
1 tsp soya sauce
1 tbsp toasted sesame oil

for the vinaigrette
1 (2½-cm/1-in) piece fresh
    root ginger, shredded
50 ml (2 fl oz) unseasoned
    rice wine vinegar
juice of 1 lime
2 tbsp vegetable oil
2 tsp soya sauce
1 tbsp toasted sesame seeds

for the salad
100 g (4 oz) shredded carrots
100 g (4 oz) thinly sliced
    cucumber
2 heads baby bok choy,
    separated into leaves
2 red peppers, deseeded and
    thinly sliced
fresh coriander, to garnish

Tear the tuna slices into small pieces and arrange in a flat dish. Whisk the root ginger, soya sauce and sesame oil together and pour over the fish. Leave to marinate while you make the vinaigrette. For the vinaigrette, whisk the root ginger, rice vinegar, lime juice, oil, soya sauce and sesame seeds together in a bowl; set aside.

Arrange mounds of carrots, cucumber, bok choy and peppers around the rim of a large platter. Mound the marinated tuna in the middle. Drizzle the vinaigrette over all and garnish with coriander. Serve immediately.

Serves 6

sashimi

see variations page 41

Easier and simpler to make than sushi, sashimi is simply raw fish cut into thin, small pieces and served with a fresh vegetable relish. Sashimi-grade indicates the freshest, best-quality fish meant to be eaten raw.

225 g (8 oz) fresh amberjack, tuna, salmon
   or trout fillet, skin removed, rinsed and
   patted dry
100 g (4 oz) freshly grated carrots

100 g (4 oz) freshly grated daikon
mizuna leaves, to garnish
soya sauce, pickled root ginger and wasabi,
   to serve

Wrap and chill the fish in the freezer for an hour or two, until it is stiff but not frozen through. With a very sharp knife, cut the fillet on the diagonal into $\frac{1}{2}$-cm- ($\frac{1}{4}$-in-) thick slices. Divide and arrange the slices on 4 plates. Arrange the grated carrots, daikon and mizuna on each plate. Serve with soya sauce, pickled root ginger and wasabi.

Serves 4

halibut crudo

see variations page 42

Crudo is the Italian version of sashimi, usually made with thinly sliced raw fish, extra-virgin olive oil, a drizzle of lemon juice and fresh herbs. Like sushi, crudo offers a wealth of choices, so feel free to create your own version. Just make sure the fish is very thinly sliced and attractive on the plate. Sashimi-grade indicates the freshest, best-quality fish meant to be eaten raw.

225 g (8 oz) sashimi-grade halibut fillet, skin removed, rinsed and patted dry
extra-virgin olive oil for drizzling

coarse kosher or sea salt
1 lemon, cut into 8 wedges
fresh basil or mint leaves, to garnish

Wrap and chill the halibut in the freezer for an hour or two, until it is stiff but not frozen through. Slice it horizontally – across the grain – into eight $\frac{1}{3}$-cm- ($\frac{1}{8}$-in-) thick pieces. Drizzle olive oil on each of 4 plates. Arrange the fish on the olive oil and sprinkle with salt. Place 2 lemon wedges on each plate and scatter fresh basil or mint leaves over all. Keep chilled before serving.

Serves 4

simple sushi

see variations page 43

To make simple sushi, you roll up bite-sized pieces of raw fish and seasoned sushi rice in roasted seaweed wrappers known as nori. You'll need a sushi mat – a small, flexible rectangle made from thin pieces of bamboo – to help you roll everything together. You make the sushi right before you're ready to serve it, as the seaweed wrappers can be tough to chew if they get soggy.

100 g (4 oz) fish fillets, such as tuna, mackerel,
    salmon or halibut, rinsed and patted dry
1 (19–22 cm/7¹/₂–8¹/₂-in) nori

100 g (4 oz) cooked sushi rice
soya sauce, pickled root ginger and prepared
    wasabi, to serve

Cut the fish into thin, finger-sized pieces. Lay a sheet of nori, shiny-side down, on the sushi mat. Gently spread the sushi rice over the wrapper, leaving a 2¹/₂-cm (1-in) border at the top. In the centre of the rice, lay a horizontal band of raw fish. Starting at the top, use the sushi mat to help you roll the sushi so that it is firm but not tight, making sure the rice does not come out at the ends. Remove the sushi roll from the mat and cut it into 8 pieces. Serve the sushi with small bowls of soya sauce, pickled root ginger and wasabi for dipping.

Serves 4

gravlax

see variations page 44

With its silken texture and fresh flavour, thinly sliced gravlax makes a wonderful appetiser or first course with buttered brown or rye bread. Gravlax is a Scandinavian specialty of fresh salmon cured in a mixture of sugar, salt and herbs for a succulent finish. Gravlax freezes well for up to 3 months.

1½ kg (3 lb) salmon fillet, preferably the centre
    cut, skin removed, rinsed and patted dry
25 g (1 oz) fine kosher salt
25 g (1 oz) sugar

175 g (6 oz) freshly chopped dill (tops
    and stems)
1 tsp freshly ground black pepper

Remove any stray bones from the fillet with tweezers. Pat the fillet dry again. Combine the salt, sugar, dill and pepper in a bowl. Rub the flesh side of the salmon with the mixture. Place salmon in a baking pan to catch the juices. Cover with clingfilm. Place a brick or a heavy tin on top of the salmon. Refrigerate for 72 hours.

When ready to serve, discard the liquid in the bottom of the pan. Scrape off most of the topping, slice the salmon very thinly on the diagonal and serve. Gravlax keeps in the refrigerator, well wrapped, for up to 1 week. If you want to freeze it, separate the slices with pieces of waxed or parchment paper, then package and freeze.

Serves 8–10

peruvian ceviche

see variations page 45

The Pacific coast of Peru is famous for its marinated raw fish dish known as ceviche. Basically, small pieces of raw fish are 'cooked' in citrus juice or vinegar enlivened with other flavourings, then served chilled in a small bowl or on ceviche spoons.

325 g (12 oz) fresh swordfish, tuna or
    mahi mahi, rinsed, patted dry and cut into
    small cubes
100 ml (4 fl oz) fresh lime juice
2 tbsp fresh orange juice
1 tsp ground cumin
salt and ground white pepper, to taste

100 g (4 oz) deseeded and finely
    chopped watermelon
50 g (2 oz) freshly grated jicama
50 g (2 oz) finely chopped green onion
50 g (2 oz) finely chopped and peeled
    ripe tomato

Put the fish in a large glass or ceramic bowl. Add the lime and orange juices, cumin, salt and white pepper. Mix well and cover tightly with clingfilm. Refrigerate for 15 minutes.

Unwrap, then stir in the watermelon, jicama, onion and tomato. Cover tightly again and refrigerate for 15 more minutes or until the fish is turning opaque on the outside but is still rare on the inside. Serve chilled.

Serves 8

snapper aotearoa

see variations page 46

Aotearoa is the Maori name for New Zealand. Of the 1,000 varieties of New Zealand saltwater fish, the best known and most prized is snapper, a favourite of recreational anglers. You can also use yellowtail kingfish, red snapper or John Dory fillets in this marinated raw fish recipe, which is perfect for replacing a prawn cocktail or for serving over salad greens.

900 g (2 lb) snapper fillets, skin
    removed, rinsed, patted dry and cut
    into 1-cm (½-in) cubes
juice of 2 lemons
juice of 1 lime
1 medium red onion, very thinly sliced
1 red or yellow pepper, deseeded and very
    thinly sliced

1 green pepper, deseeded and very
    thinly sliced
225 g (8 oz) cherry tomatoes, stems removed
    and cut in half
1 (400-g/14-oz) tin coconut milk
fine sea salt, to taste

Place the cubed fish in a glass or ceramic bowl. Squeeze the citrus juice over the fish. Cover with clingfilm and leave to stand in the refrigerator until the fish whitens, about 4–8 hours. Stir in the vegetables and coconut milk. Add salt, to taste. Serve in cocktail glasses or over salad leaves.

Serves 6

tuna tartare in tortilla cones

see variations page 47

Simple raw fish recipes like this one allow you time to create a more interesting presentation. The small tortilla cones are easy to make. See the recipes on page 47 for even more colourful and interesting presentation ideas, like contemporary paintings on a plate.

4 (25-cm/10-in) flour tortillas
100 g (4 oz) tuna steak, skin removed, rinsed, patted dry and finely chopped
2 plum tomatoes, deseeded and finely chopped
1 green onion, finely chopped

50 ml (2 fl oz) fresh lime juice
50 g (2 oz) finely chopped fresh coriander
2 tsp vegetable oil
1/4 tsp bottled hot pepper sauce

Preheat the oven to 175°C (350°F/Gas mark 4). Using a 7½-cm (3-in) round biscuit cutter, cut 5 circles from each tortilla. Form each circle into a cone, securing the base with a toothpick. Place on a baking tray and bake for 10 minutes or until lightly browned and crisp. Leave to cool.

For the tartare, combine the remaining ingredients in a glass or ceramic bowl and gently stir to blend. Cover and chill for 1 to 24 hours. To serve, drain excess juice from the tartare. Spoon the tartare into each cone and serve on a platter.

Serves 4

variations

oysters on the half shell

see base recipe page 23

scallops on the half shell
Prepare basic recipe, using sea scallops in place of oysters.

oysters with pickled root ginger, wasabi & miso-soya sauce
Replace mignonette sauce with miso-soya dipping sauce. In saucepan, whisk
25 g (1 oz) packed brown sugar, 2 tablespoons soya sauce, 2 tablespoons hot
water and 2 tablespoons miso. Boil, then chill for 2 hours. Prepare oysters, and
add 1 tablespoon pickled root ginger and 1 teaspoon prepared wasabi to
each plate.

oysters with horseradish sauce
Replace mignonette sauce with horseradish sauce. Whisk 225 ml (8 fl oz)
ketchup, 2 tablespoons prepared horseradish, ½ teaspoon bottled hot pepper
sauce, ½ teaspoon Worcestershire sauce and 1 tablespoon fresh lime juice.

Barbecued oysters with salsa verde
Instead of basic recipe, whisk 225 g (8 oz) tinned tomatillos, 25 g (1 oz) finely
chopped green onion, 1 finely chopped jalapeño (deseeded), 2 teaspoons fresh
lime juice and salt, to taste. Preheat the barbecue. Drizzle each oyster on half
shell with salsa verde, place on barbecue rack, cover and barbecue 3–4 minutes
or until oyster edges begin to curl. Garnish with limes.

variations

fresh tuna carpaccio

see base recipe page 24

fresh salmon carpaccio
Prepare the basic recipe, using fresh salmon in place of tuna.

fresh tuna carpaccio with ginger-lime sauce
Prepare the basic recipe, but replace the carpaccio sauce with ginger-lime sauce.
Whisk 175 g (6 oz) mayonnaise with 2 tablespoons fresh lime juice, 2 tablespoons
grated fresh root ginger and ¼ teaspoon bottled hot sauce. Omit the capers.

fresh salmon carpaccio with aïoli
Prepare the basic recipe, using salmon in place of tuna and Aïoli (page 262)
in place of carpaccio sauce. Use finely chopped, pitted Kalamata olives in
place of capers.

fresh tuna carpaccio-san
Prepare the basic recipe, but instead of the carpaccio sauce, whisk together
50 g (2 oz) tahini, 50 ml (2 fl oz) unseasoned rice wine vinegar, 25 g (1 oz)
wasabi powder, 1½ teaspoons Dijon mustard, 1½ teaspoons brown sugar and
1 tablespoon soya sauce. Omit capers.

variations

asian raw fish salad

see base recipe page 27

asian raw fish salad with pickled root ginger

Prepare the basic recipe, adding 100 g (4 oz) pickled root ginger to the platter of salad ingredients.

asian raw salmon salad

Prepare the basic recipe, using salmon cut in the carpaccio style (page 24) in place of tuna.

asian smoked salmon salad

Prepare the basic recipe, using thin slices of smoked salmon in place of raw tuna.

asian raw fish salad with plum vinaigrette & wonton crisps

Prepare the basic recipe, adding 2 teaspoons Chinese plum sauce to the vinaigrette. Add 50 g (2 oz) wonton crisps or chow mein noodles and 100 g (4 oz) pickled root ginger to the salad ingredients.

sashimi

see base recipe page 28

seared sashimi
Instead of basic recipe, brush top of chilled fillet with 1 tablespoon canola oil. Heat a cast-iron frying pan until very hot, add fish, oiled-side down, and sear for 1 minute. Slice thinly on diagonal and serve with lemon.

sashimi with hot sesame oil
Prepare basic recipe, omitting garnish. Arrange fish slices on 4 plates. Drizzle fish with juice of 1 orange and sprinkle with matchstick slices of fresh root ginger. Heat 2 tablespoons canola oil and 1 teaspoon toasted sesame oil and drizzle over the fish. Top with chopped coriander.

sashimi with garlic-soya sauce
Prepare basic recipe. Bring to the boil 3 tablespoons soya sauce, 1 tablespoon unseasoned rice wine vinegar, 1½ teaspoons sugar, ½ teaspoon grated fresh root ginger, 4 small minced cloves garlic, 1 teaspoon vegetable oil and ½ teaspoon bottled hot sauce. Cool and serve as a dipping sauce.

squid sashimi
Instead of fillet, use 4 medium sashimi-grade squid, filleted and skinned. Wrap and freeze for 30 minutes until firm, slice thinly on the diagonal and proceed with basic recipe.

variations

halibut crudo

see base recipe page 30

bay scallop crudo
Prepare the basic recipe, using small scallops in place of halibut (no need to cut into smaller pieces) and fresh chervil or tarragon in place of the basil.

halibut crudo with pesto
Prepare the basic recipe, drizzling the raw fish with prepared pesto. Garnish with lemon wedges and fresh basil leaves.

swordfish crudo with tapenade
Prepare the basic recipe, using swordfish in place of halibut. Drizzle the raw fish with prepared tapenade. Garnish with lemon wedges and finely chopped, pitted Kalamata olives.

halibut crudo with lemon & black pepper
Prepare the basic recipe, adding a grating of fresh lemon zest and a sprinkling of black pepper on top of each serving.

salmon crudo with carpaccio sauce
Prepare the basic recipe, using salmon in place of halibut and flat-leaf parsley leaves instead of basil. Drizzle the raw fish with carpaccio sauce (page 24).

variations

simple sushi

see base recipe page 31

easy california roll
Instead of basic recipe, lay a sheet of clingfilm over the sushi mat and spread 100 g (4 oz) sushi rice into a 18-cm (7-in) square. Lay a sheet of nori, shiny-side up, on top of the rice, leaving a 2½-cm (1-in) border on top. Across the middle, lay a band of finger-sized pieces of avocado. Lay a band of cooked crabmeat on the avocado. Using sushi mat and clingfilm, start rolling sushi into a log, removing the clingfilm as you go. Cut into 8 pieces and serve.

cucumber sushi
Prepare basic recipe, adding finger-sized pieces of cucumber next to the raw fish.

asparagus & prawn sushi
Prepare basic recipe, using large cooked prawns in place of raw fish and adding finger-sized pieces of steamed asparagus.

finger or 'nigiri' sushi
Prepare basic recipe, omitting nori. Place 25 g (1 oz) sushi rice in one hand. Add a small piece of raw fish. Dab fish with the wasabi. With your hands, cover fish with rice and form a cylinder shape. Repeat with the remaining fish and rice.

variations

gravlax

see base recipe page 32

dill & beet-cured gravlax
Prepare the basic recipe, adding 100 g (4 oz) shredded beets and 1 teaspoon ground coriander to the topping ingredients.

seared gravlax
Prepare the basic recipe. After removing the gravlax from the refrigerator and brushing off most but not all of the topping, brush the top with 1 tablespoon canola oil. Heat a cast-iron frying pan until very hot. Place the gravlax, topping-side down, in the hot pan and sear for 1 minute. Slice on the diagonal and serve with lemon wedges.

gravlax with juniper berries
Prepare the basic recipe, adding 25 g (1 oz) crushed juniper berries to the topping.

orange-zested gravlax
Prepare the basic recipe, adding 2 teaspoons grated fresh orange zest and 1 teaspoon grated fresh lemon zest to the topping.

peruvian ceviche

see base recipe page 34

fresh tilapia ceviche
Prepare the basic recipe, using fresh tilapia.

fresh tuna ceviche
Prepare the basic recipe, using sashimi-grade tuna, chopped avocado in place of the watermelon and freshly chopped coriander leaves in place of the green onion.

prawn chipotle ceviche
Prepare the basic recipe, using 8 raw, peeled and deveined medium-sized prawns, cut into 1-cm (½-in) pieces, in place of the fish; 2 chipotle tinned chillies in adobo sauce, chopped, in place of the watermelon; and freshly chopped coriander in place of the onion.

lobster, poblano & mango ceviche
Prepare the basic recipe, using 4 fresh or frozen and thawed lobster tails – cooked in boiling water for 3 minutes or until the shells turn red, and then chopped – in place of the fish; 2 pitted and chopped mangoes in place of the watermelon; 1 poblano chilli – roasted, stemmed, deseeded and chopped – in place of the tomatoes; and freshly chopped coriander in place of the onion.

variations

snapper aotearoa

see base recipe page 35

samoan snapper
Prepare the basic recipe, using the juice of 3 fresh lemons in place of lemon and lime juice, and 25 g (1 oz) finely chopped green onions in place of the red onion. Garnish with thin slices of lemon.

Barbecued snapper aotearoa
Prepare the basic recipe, but leave the snapper fillets whole. Brush with vegetable oil on each side and barbecue over a high heat for about 3½ minutes on each side, turning once. Stir together the citrus juices, vegetables, coconut milk and salt, to taste. Serve the fish in a pool of the sauce.

thai-style snapper
Prepare the basic recipe, replacing the 2 lemons with 1 or 2 more limes. Instead of the vegetables, stir 1 small deseeded and chopped red or green serrano pepper and 1 tablespoon green curry paste with the coconut milk. Garnish with chopped fresh coriander.

orange grove snapper
Prepare the basic recipe, using the zest and juice of 1 orange in place of the juice of 1 lime. Garnish with chopped fresh coriander.

tuna tartare in tortilla cones

see base recipe page 36

tartare trio
Omit tortilla cones. In place of the tuna, place 50 g (2 oz) finely chopped
tilapia, 50 g (2 oz) finely chopped salmon and 50 g (2 oz) finely chopped
monkfish in each of 3 glass or ceramic bowls. Combine remaining
ingredients, then divide among the 3 bowls of fish. Cover and chill from 1 to
24 hours, then drain off excess liquid. Place a mound of each tartare on each
plate and garnish with fresh chopped coriander.

salmon tartare
Prepare basic recipe, replacing flour tortillas with green jalapeño-flavoured
tortillas and tuna with salmon.

bay scallop tartare
Prepare basic recipe, replacing flour tortillas with red chile-flavoured tortillas
and tuna with 100 g (4 oz) small scallops.

tartare tower
Prepare the basic recipe, omitting the tortilla cones. Spoon the tartare into
4–6 ramekins; cover and chill up to 24 hours. To serve, drain off excess liquid
from each ramekin. Carefully invert in the centre of each plate. Drizzle
Mango & Lime Salsa (page 265) around the perimeter of each plate and
garnish with chopped coriander.

all steamed up

Since Neolithic times, simple steaming, poaching,

and boiling have been favoured cooking methods

for fish and seafood. For a moist, succulent result,

cook just until the fish is opaque or the shellfish has

turned pale pink. Add colour and texture with a

variety of classic sauces from around the world.

classic prawn cocktail

see variations page 64

To take a prawn cocktail from ho-hum to wow involves just a little more work on the part of the cook. Get the best flavour by starting with whole, head-on prawns and cook them yourself. Mix up classic cocktail sauce in a few seconds, then serve it all chilled.

1 L (4 pt) water
25 g (1 oz) kosher or table salt
450 g (1 lb) large prawns, deveined, shell on,
    with heads intact, rinsed, and patted dry
crisp lettuce leaves, to serve

for the classic cocktail sauce
225 ml (8 fl oz) tomato ketchup
prepared horseradish, to taste
fresh lemon juice, to taste
bottled hot sauce, to taste

In a large saucepan, combine water and salt and bring to the boil. Add the prawns. Cover and cook for 6–8 minutes or until the prawns are pink and just opaque. Check periodically and do not overcook. Remove from the cooking water and leave to stand in very cold water to stop the cooking. When cool enough to handle, twist off the head and pull off the legs of each prawn. Hold the tail and lift the shell upward to peel. Use a small knife to remove the black vein (the digestive tract). Rinse under cold water, then cover and chill until ready to serve.

Whisk the cocktail sauce ingredients together in a small bowl. Cover and refrigerate until ready to serve. To serve, arrange crisp lettuce leaves on each plate or in a cocktail glass. Top with prawns and cocktail sauce.

Serves 4

steamed crab

see variations page 65

Live crabs steamed in a flavourful liquid can be picked and eaten with melted butter right then and there. The picked meat can also be used in lump form in salads or crab cakes; flaked crabmeat is more suitable for dips and fillings. While it's easy to steam crab, it's more difficult to pick out the meat – that's why crabmeat is expensive to buy already picked. But once you get the hang of it, you're fine.

1 dozen live crabs
225 ml (8 fl oz) cider vinegar
225 ml (8 fl oz) beer

3 tbsp sea salt
1 tbsp crab seasoning

Make sure that all the crabs are alive; discard any that do not move. Bring the vinegar, beer, salt and seasoning to the boil in a large steamer (or a saucepan with a wire rack placed in the bottom to keep crabs from touching the boiling water). Cover, reduce heat to simmer and steam for 20–25 minutes or until all the crabs are bright orange. Transfer the crabs to a newspaper-covered flat surface. Have ready a bowl for the crabmeat, a bowl for the good shells and a rubbish bin. When cool enough to handle, take one crab and turn it smooth shell-side down. Pull off the legs and claws; set them aside. Pull off the narrow and pointy (male crab) or wide, triangular (female) plate. Turn the crab on its side. Wedge your thumbs between the smooth shell and the body and pull apart. Remove anything that is not fine, white crabmeat. Break the body in half and pick out the crabmeat. Crack the claws and legs with pliers and extract more meat. Save the larger shells to make shellfish stock. Serve the picked crab with melted butter.

Serves 4

mussels steamed in white wine, garlic & herbs

see variations page 66

One of the classic dishes of Belgium served with frites and homemade mayonnaise, steamed mussels are easy to make and delicious to eat. Make sure you scrub away the 'beard' from each mussel. Discard any that are open before you steam them and any that don't open after steaming.

1 tbsp olive oil
1 medium onion, chopped
2 cloves garlic, thinly sliced
225 ml (8 fl oz) dry white wine
1 tbsp chopped fresh tarragon

1½ kg (3 lb) mussels, scrubbed, with
    beards removed
50 g (2 oz) chopped fresh Italian parsley,
    to garnish

Place the oil in a large saucepan and sauté the onion and garlic over medium-high heat until transparent, about 4 minutes. Pour in the wine, add the tarragon and heat to boiling. Add the mussels, cover and cook for 5–7 minutes or until the shells open, shaking the pot occasionally. Discard any unopened mussels. To serve, ladle the mussels and their broth into 6 large soup bowls and garnish with parsley.

Serves 6

thai seafood & vegetable wraps

see variations page 67

Colourful, delicious, and easy to make, these see-through wraps show off the ingredients. Serve with a dipping sauce for appetisers or a light lunch.

50 ml (2 fl oz) soya sauce
1 tbsp honey
1 tsp toasted sesame oil
1/2 tsp black sesame seeds
1 clove garlic, minced
50 g (2 oz) rice sticks
225 g (8 oz) peeled and deveined cooked
    prawns, coarsely chopped

50 ml (2 fl oz) unseasoned rice wine vinegar
1 1/2 tsp grated fresh root ginger
50 g (2 oz) grated carrots
25 g (1 oz) chopped fresh mint
2 green onions, thinly sliced
8 (20-cm/8 1/2-in) rice paper wraps
100 g (4 oz) shredded romaine lettuce

Whisk the soya sauce, honey, sesame oil, sesame seeds and minced garlic together in a small bowl. Cook the rice sticks in enough boiling water to cover for 2–3 minutes or until tender. Drain and rinse with cold water. Drain again and snap rick sticks into bite-sized pieces. In a small bowl, combine the prawns, vinegar and root ginger. In another bowl, combine the carrots, mint and green onions.

Dip one rice paper wrap at a time into a shallow bowl of warm water. Shake off extra water and lay flat between clean, damp kitchen towels. Leave to stand for 3–4 minutes or until pliable. Lay out each rice paper wrapper on a flat surface. Layer lettuce, rice sticks, prawn mixture and carrot mixture. Carefully roll up into a cylinder, folding in the sides as you go. Cut the wraps in half on the diagonal and serve with the dipping sauce.

Serves 8

singapore-style steamed fish in banana leaves

see variations page 68

Wrapping fish and its flavourings in banana leaves, then steaming, produces a tender, aromatic result. Fish fillets steam the quickest, but you can also do this with small, whole, cleaned fish – just allow 15 or 20 minutes more. You can buy frozen banana leaves in packages at Hispanic markets or in some supermarkets. Just thaw, cut to size and wrap the fish. If you can't find banana leaves, you can use aluminium foil.

50 g (2 oz) dessicated (not sweetened, flaked) coconut
175 ml (6 fl oz) hot water
1 clove garlic
1 tbsp freshly grated ginger
$\frac{1}{4}$ tsp ground root ginger
1 tsp ground coriander

1 tsp garam masala or curry powder
1 tsp fine sea salt
$1\frac{1}{2}$ tbsp fresh lemon juice
1 tbsp chopped fresh coriander leaves
4 tilapia, cod or halibut fillets, skin removed, rinsed and patted dry
1 large banana leaf, cut in pieces

In a food processor, process the coconut, water, garlic, fresh and ground root ginger, coriander, garam masala, salt and lemon juice until very finely ground. Stir in the coriander leaves. Place each fish fillet in the centre of a banana leaf or piece of foil big enough to completely enclose it. Top the fish fillet with a quarter of the coconut mixture, then wrap up in the banana leaf or piece of foil. Fill a steamer with water. Bring to the boil. Place the wrapped fish fillets, seam-side down, in a single layer in the steamer basket or on the rack. Cover and steam for 15 minutes or until fish begins to flake when tested with a fork in the thickest part of the fillet. Unwrap and eat.
Serves 4

chinese seafood dumplings

see variations page 69

Dumplings of all kinds help celebrate Chinese New Year, usually in February. But these are delicious any time and great for appetisers or dim sum. This recipe makes several dozen dumplings, but they'll all be gone in a hurry. You can use either fresh or frozen raw prawns.

450 g (1 lb) medium raw prawns, peeled and
   deveined, rinsed and patted dry
2 green onions, coarsely chopped
1 tbsp coarsely chopped fresh coriander
1 tbsp coarsely chopped fresh mint
2 tsp soya sauce
fine sea salt, to taste
2 tbsp double cream

54 (9-cm/3½-in diameter) round
   dumpling wrappers, gyoza skins or
   pot sticker wrappers
1 large egg, beaten with 2 tbsp water
Asian Vinaigrette (page 27), Miso-Soya Sauce
   (page 38), and/or Garlic-Soya Sauce
   (page 41) for dipping

In a food processor, pulse the prawns, green onions, coriander, mint and soya sauce together until finely chopped. Season to taste. Transfer the mixture to a bowl and stir in the cream. Arrange the wrappers on a flat surface. Brush the egg mixture around the perimeter of each wrapper. Place a rounded teaspoon of filling in the centre, then fold wrapper into a half-moon shape and press the edges together to seal.

Bring a large saucepan of water to the boil. Add the dumplings in batches, and cook until the skins turn transparent and the prawns are pink, about 2 minutes. Drain in a colander and serve warm with a dipping sauce.

Serves 8–10

classic poached salmon

see variations page 70

Pale coral-coloured poached salmon on a platter is delicious for a breakfast, brunch, lunch, dinner or a festive meal of little plates. Hollandaise (page 264) is the classic sauce to serve with it, but many other sauces are also delicious accompaniments.

900 g (2 lb) salmon fillet, skin on and any
    bones removed, rinsed and patted dry
fine sea salt
ground white pepper
lemon slices, watercress, and cucumber slices,
    to garnish

for the salmon stock
3½ L (6 pt) water
225 ml (8 fl oz) dry white wine
100 ml (4 fl oz) tarragon vinegar
225 g (8 oz) chopped carrots
225 g (8 oz) chopped onions
6 fresh parsley stalks
2 bay leaves
1 tbsp whole black peppercorns

Preheat the oven to 230°C (450°F/Gas mark 8). Season the salmon fillet, wrap in a double layer of muslin and place in a large buttered baking dish. Bring the water to the boil in a large pot, then stir in the wine, vinegar, carrots, onions, parsley stalks, bay leaves and peppercorns. Simmer for 15 minutes. Carefully pour the stock over the salmon so it reaches three-quarters of the way up the fillet. Poach in the oven for 7–8 minutes. Remove from the oven and allow salmon to cool in the stock. When cool enough to handle, remove salmon from the stock, remove muslin from the salmon and place the salmon on a serving platter. Garnish with lemon and cucumber slices and watercress sprigs. Serve warm or cover and chill to serve later. Strain the stock, leave to cool to room temperature, then freeze for another use.

Serves 4

butter-poached lobster

see variations page 71

Butter poaching is a gentle way to get the maximum flavour from previously frozen (cooked and thawed) seafood. The poaching liquid can then be flavoured with a variety of ingredients to make interesting sauces.

8 small frozen and thawed rock lobster tails
    and/or claws
lemon juice, to taste
kosher or sea salt and ground white pepper,
    to taste
4 tbsp unsalted butter

50 ml (2 fl oz) chicken stock, shellfish stock
    (page 65) or salmon stock (page 58)
50 ml (2 fl oz) dry white wine
50 ml (2 fl oz) dry white vermouth, port
    or sherry
50 ml (2 fl oz) double cream

Preheat oven to 200°C (400°F/Gas mark 6). Gently remove the lobster meat from the shell to keep it all in once piece. Drizzle with lemon juice and season with salt and white pepper. Heat the butter in a heavy casserole dish (with a lid) until bubbling. Quickly roll the lobster meat in the hot butter, then top the casserole dish with a round of greaseproof paper, cover with the lid and place in the oven for 6–8 minutes or until lobster meat is white and springy to the touch.

Remove casserole dish from the oven. Transfer the lobster to a platter and keep warm. Place the casserole dish over high heat and stir in the stock and white wine. Reduce until the liquid is syrupy, about 5 minutes. Whisk in the vermouth and bring to the boil. Cook for 1 minute. Whisk in the cream. Taste for seasoning and serve the sauce over the lobster.

Serves 4

easy paella

see variations page 72

Paella is a great party dish and this version takes only about 45 minutes to prepare.

2 tbsp olive oil
100 g (4 oz) chopped onion
50 g (2 oz) chopped red pepper
50 g (2 oz) chopped green pepper
4 garlic cloves, minced
1 bay leaf
450 g (1 lb) chopped tinned tomatoes,
    with juices
½ tsp saffron threads or 1 tbsp paprika

450 g (1 lb) short-grain, risotto or paella rice
1 L (2 pt) chicken stock or salmon stock
    (page 58)
8 clams, scrubbed
8 mussels, scrubbed, beards removed
8 peeled and deveined large raw prawns, rinsed
    and patted dry
100 g (4 oz) frozen peas, thawed
chopped fresh Italian parsley, to garnish

Heat the olive oil in a large paella pan or large saucepan. Sauté the onion, peppers and garlic over medium-high heat until softened, about 5 minutes. Add the bay leaf, tomatoes, saffron and rice, and cook, stirring, for 2 minutes. Add the chicken stock and bring to the boil. Reduce the heat, cover and simmer for 15–20 minutes or until the rice is almost tender. Add the clams, mussels and prawns, cover and simmer for 10 minutes or until the clams and mussels have opened and the prawns are pink and opaque. Stir in the peas until warmed through. Serve garnished with Italian parsley.

Serves 8

seashore lobster dinner

see variations page 73

This one-pot meal – cooked outdoors over a barbecue or indoors on the hob – conjures up summers at the seaside. Spread layers of newspapers over the table for the traditional (and easy) clean-up. Place the contents of the saucepan in the middle of the table and it's all hands on deck.

4 live (450-g/1-lb) lobsters
450 g (1 lb) trimmed string beans

kernels from 4 corn cobs
Sesame Mayonnaise (page 275)

Bring a large saucepan of salted water to the boil. Add the lobsters, cover and cook for 8 minutes or until starting to turn red in places. Add the string beans and corn and cook, covered, until the beans are almost crisp-tender and the lobsters have turned completely red, about 4 more minutes. Drain the pan and turn out the contents on a newspaper-covered table. Serve with Sesame Mayonnaise.

Serves 4

variations

classic prawn cocktail

see base recipe page 49

simple boiled crawfish
Prepare basic recipe, using crawfish in place of prawns and adding Cajun
seasoning to taste to cocktail sauce. Before cooking, soak the live crawfish in a
mixture of 925 ml (32 fl oz) cold water and 100 g (4 oz) salt for 2 hours so they
expel any mud. Drain and rinse before boiling.

smoked prawn cocktail
Prepare an indirect fire in the barbecue. Make an aluminium foil packet, place a
large handful of wood chips in it, close packet and poke several holes in top.
Place packet on the coals or near a gas jet. Arrange prawns in a disposable foil
pan, brush with olive oil and place on indirect (no heat) side. At the first wisp of
smoke, close lid. Smoke prawns for 30 minutes or until pink and almost opaque.
Proceed with recipe.

classic prawn cocktail with mango lime sauce
Prepare basic recipe, using Mango & Lime Salsa (page 265) in place of
cocktail sauce.

crab cocktail
Prepare basic recipe, using crabmeat in place of prawns.

variations

steamed crab

see base recipe page 50

steamed lobster
Prepare basic recipe, using 4 live lobsters instead of crab. Steam for 20–25 minutes or until they turn red. Pick apart like crab and serve with melted butter.

shellfish stock
Roast 1–1¹/₂ kg (2–3 lb) of steamed, cracked crab, prawn or lobster shells on baking tray for 10 minutes at 200°C (400°F/Gas mark 6). Put shells in large saucepan, cover with water, bring to a simmer. For 20 minutes, skim away foam on surface. Add 225 ml (8 fl oz) dry white wine, 1 chopped onion, 100 g (4 oz) chopped celery, 100 g (4 oz) chopped carrot, 1 bay leaf, 1 tablespoon tomato paste and 1 teaspoon dried thyme. For 30 minutes, skim off foam. Remove from heat; strain through double layers of muslin. Do not press on shells. Discard solids. Season to taste. Freeze in ¹/₂-litre measures. Makes 2¹/₂ litres (4 pints).

easy crab salad
Combine 325 g (12 oz) lump crabmeat with 1 tablespoon Dijon mustard, 100 g (4 oz) mayonnaise, 1 tablespoon fresh dill, salt and white pepper. Serve chilled.

steamed crab with ginger–lime sauce
Prepare basic recipe, using Ginger–Lime Sauce (page 39) in place of melted butter.

mussels steamed in white wine, garlic & herbs

see base recipe page 53

mussels steamed in white wine & saffron
Prepare basic recipe, using ½ teaspoon saffron threads in place of tarragon.

mussels steamed in beer
Prepare basic recipe, using 1 (325-g/12-oz) bottle of beer in place of wine and tarragon.

steamed clams with casino butter
Prepare basic recipe, using clams in place of mussels. To make Casino Butter, mix 4 strips crisp and crumbled bacon, 8 tablespoons softened butter, 50 g (2 oz) finely chopped green onions, bottled hot sauce to taste, 1 teaspoon Worcestershire sauce, 50 ml (2 fl oz) fresh lemon juice, salt, and pepper. Toast slices of French bread. Serve each bowl of clams with slices of bread and Casino Butter.

sake-steamed clams
Prepare the basic recipe, using clams in place of mussels. In place of wine, garlic and herbs, use 100 ml (4 fl oz) sake, 100 ml (4 fl oz) mirin and 1 tablespoon unseasoned rice vinegar. Cover and steam clams until opened, then transfer to bowls. Stir 2 chopped green onions, 2 tablespoons soya sauce and 6 tablespoons butter into steaming liquid, then ladle liquid over clams.

thai seafood & vegetable wraps

see base recipe page 54

thai fish & vegetable wraps
Prepare basic recipe, using 325 g (12 oz) cooked fish in place of prawns.

thai seafood & vegetable wraps with two sauces
Prepare basic recipe, using salmon in place of prawns and adding Mango & Lime Salsa (page 265) as another dipping sauce.

baja seafood & vegetable wraps
Prepare basic recipe, using 25-cm (10-in) flour tortillas in place of rice paper wraps, 1 chopped avocado in place of rice sticks, 1 tablespoon bottled chipotle sauce in place of fresh root ginger and coriander in place of mint. Serve with more bottled chipotle sauce in place of dipping sauce.

indonesian prawn & peanut wraps with papaya lime sauce
Combine cooked prawns, root ginger and green onion. Instead of rice sticks, carrots and mint, stir in 100 g (4 oz) finely chopped salted roasted peanuts, 1 tablespoon fish sauce, 2 tablespoons sweet chilli sauce and 50 g (1 oz) chopped coriander. Stir in the romaine. Spoon mixture onto each rice paper wrap and roll up. Add Papaya & Lime Salsa (page 277) as a dipping sauce.

variations

singapore-style steamed fish in banana leaves

see base recipe page 56

singapore-style baked fish in banana leaves
Prepare basic recipe, but instead of steaming, bake fish on a baking tray at 175°C (350°F/Gas mark 4) for 15 minutes.

rainforest fish in banana leaves
Prepare basic recipe, using farm-raised catfish in place of tilapia, ground chipotle in place of garam masala and fresh lime juice in place of lemon. Omit fresh and ground root ginger.

chinese-style fish steamed in banana leaves
Lightly brush fillets with toasted sesame oil and top with 50 g (2 oz) chopped mushrooms. Drizzle with 1 tablespoon soya sauce. Sprinkle with 2 chopped green onions and 2 tablespoons chopped fresh coriander. Wrap in banana leaves and proceed with recipe.

plated perch
Butter inside of a large heatproof plate and arrange perch fillets on it in a single layer. Sprinkle with salt and ground white pepper and drizzle with 2 tablespoons each dry white wine and fresh lemon juice. Invert a second buttered plate over fish. Place plated fish over a pan of boiling water and steam for 15 minutes.

chinese seafood dumplings

see base recipe page 57

chinese crabmeat dumplings
Prepare basic recipe, using 450 g (1 lb) lump crabmeat in place of prawns.

seafood wontons
Prepare basic recipe, using wonton wrappers in place of dumpling wrappers.
Moisten the perimeter of each wrapper with the egg mixture, fold the
wrapper over the filling to form a triangle and press the edges together to
seal. Fry in hot oil, in batches, until golden brown.

crab rangoon
Instead of basic recipe, make Crab Rangoon in wonton wrappers. In a food
processor, pulse 225 g (8 oz) cream cheese; 225 g (8 oz) cooked crabmeat,
drained and flaked; $1/2$ teaspoon Worcestershire sauce; $1/2$ teaspoon soya
sauce; 2 finely chopped green onions; 1 minced garlic clove; and ground
white pepper, to taste. Moisten the perimeter of wonton wrappers with
diluted egg, fold wrapper over filling to form a triangle and press edges
together to seal. Fry in hot oil, in batches, until golden brown.

chinese salmon dumplings
Prepare the basic recipe, using raw salmon in place of prawns.

variations

classic poached salmon

see base recipe page 58

poached halibut
Prepare basic recipe, using halibut in place of salmon.

poached salmon aïoli platter
Prepare basic recipe. Serve salmon on a platter, surrounded by cured black olives, artichoke hearts, baby carrots, steamed thin green beans and cherry tomatoes. Serve Aïoli (page 262) on the side.

traditional aïoli platter
Prepare basic recipe, using dried, salted cod in place of salmon. Three days before poaching, soak salted cod in water. Cover and refrigerate. Each day, drain off salty water, add fresh cold water, cover and refrigerate. When the cod is firm but rehydrated, proceed with recipe. Serve the cod on a platter as in the variation above.

classic cold poached salmon with herbed tomato vinaigrette
Prepare basic recipe. Place poached salmon on a platter, cover and chill. Serve with Herbed Tomato Vinaigrette (page 258).

variations

butter-poached lobster

see base recipe page 60

butter-poached prawns
Prepare basic recipe, using raw prawns in place of lobster and poaching
3–4 minutes until prawns are opaque and pink.

butter-poached lobster with blood orange sauce
Prepare basic recipe, omitting vermouth and cream. When the lobster
is done, carefully transfer to 4 plates. Place the pan over high heat and
cook until the butter begins to brown. Remove from heat and stir in
2 tablespoons fresh blood orange juice. Pour the sauce over the lobster
and serve.

butter-poached fish fillets with pernod butter sauce
Follow directions of variation above, using Pernod instead of blood
orange juice.

butter-poached fish steaks
Prepare basic recipe, using fish steaks in place of lobsters. Poach for
6–8 minutes or until opaque all the way through and springy to the touch.

variations

easy paella

see base recipe page 61

cartagena-style paella
Prepare the basic recipe, adding 8 bone-in chicken thighs. Brown the chicken in the olive oil before sautéing the vegetables, then remove from the pan. Return the chicken to the pan after the rice goes in and proceed with the recipe.

puerto rican paella
Prepare the basic recipe, adding 8 previously browned bone-in chicken thighs and 1 tablespoon Sazon seasoning with the saffron. Proceed with the recipe. Stir in 50 g (2 oz) chopped, pimento-stuffed olives with the peas and garnish with chopped fresh coriander in place of parsley.

peruvian prawn & almond paella
Prepare the basic recipe, using all prawns. Just before serving, sprinkle 50 g (2 oz) toasted, slivered almonds over the paella and fluff with a fork.

sonoran paella
Prepare the basic recipe, brown 2 links of chorizo, sliced, in the olive oil before sautéing the vegetables, then remove from the pan. Return the chorizo to the pan after the rice goes in and proceed with the recipe.

variations

seashore lobster dinner

see base recipe page 62

clam bake
Instead of basic recipe, cook 450 g (1 lb) small new potatoes in a large saucepan of water until they can almost be pierced with a fork. Then add 2 kg (4 lb) clams and kernels from 4 corn cobs. Cover and cook until clams open. Serve with melted butter.

frogmore stew
Prepare basic recipe, using headless, deveined prawns in place of lobster and adding 1 bottle of beer and 1½ tablespoons crab seasoning to the water. Cook beans first, until almost tender. Then add prawns and corn. Cover and cook until prawns are pink and opaque.

soul succotash
Prepare basic recipe, using headless, deveined prawns in place of lobster and adding 2 bottles of beer to the water. Cook beans first, until almost tender. Then add prawns, corn and 450 g (1 lb) sliced smoked sausage. Cover and cook until prawns are pink and opaque.

crab boil
Prepare basic recipe, using live crabs in place of lobster and 1½ tablespoons crab seasoning to the water. Serve with melted butter instead of Sesame Mayonnaise.

simmered

From the famous bouillabaisse from the south of France, to the clam chowders of New England and the exotic coconut-and-curry-enriched soups of southeast Asia, a slowly simmered fish soup or stew can be a meal in itself.

provençal fish soup with rouille

see variations page 90

Known as bouillabaisse in Marseilles, this seafood soup has many different versions. Most contain certain ingredients – the freshest fish and shellfish, saffron, aromatic orange peel and fennel and garlic.

50 ml (2 fl oz) olive oil
6 cloves garlic, minced
225 g (8 oz) chopped onion
100 g (4 oz) chopped bulb fennel
450 g (1 lb) tinned tomatoes with their liquid
½ tsp saffron threads
1 tsp grated orange zest or dried orange peel
1 tsp dried thyme
450 g (1 lb) small, bony fish (rascasse, red mullet, drum, and/or bream), heads removed, cut into 7-cm (3-in) pieces, rinsed and patted dry

450 g (1 lb) meaty fish (John Dory, monkfish, Pacific cod, or halibut), cleaned, heads removed, cut into 7-cm (3-in) pieces, rinsed and patted dry
450 g (1 lb) shellfish, such as shell-on prawns, clams, bay scallops and/or langoustines
rouille (page 275)
buttered and oven-toasted slices of French bread

Heat the olive oil in a large saucepan over medium-high heat. Sauté the garlic, onion and fennel until the onion is transparent, about 5 minutes. Stir in the tomatoes, saffron, orange zest, thyme and bony and meaty fish pieces. Add enough water to cover. When the water comes to the boil again, cover and simmer for 10 minutes. Add the shellfish, bring to the simmer again, cover, and simmer for an additional 10 minutes. To serve, ladle the soup into large bowls and serve with toasted bread and rouille.

Serves 6–8

clam chowder

see variations page 91

New England-style clam chowder starts with a hearty base of salt pork or bacon, and is
finished to a creamy turn.

1 slice smoked bacon, minced	1 (190-g/6½-oz) tin clams with juice
½ tsp butter	1 tbsp plain flour
225 g (8 oz) minced onion	325 ml (12 fl oz) whipping or single cream
1 garlic clove, minced	¼ tsp ground white pepper
½ tsp each: dried parsley, dill, basil, tarragon	2 medium potatoes, boiled, peeled and diced
and rosemary	

In a large saucepan, sauté the bacon, butter, onion, garlic and dried herbs over a low heat.
Do not allow to brown. Drain clams and set aside, reserving the juice. Slowly stir the flour
and clam juices into the sauté mixture. Bring to the boil; reduce heat. Add cream and simmer
for 20 minutes. Add white pepper, potatoes and clams. Heat to serving temperature, but do
not boil, as this toughens the clams. Serve at once with savoury biscuits.

Serves 4

classic lobster bisque

see variations page 92

Long a dish signifying fine dining, lobster bisque takes time to make, but the rich flavour is well worth the effort.

2 (450-g/1-lb) steamed lobsters (page 62)
100 g (4 oz) onion, diced
50 g (2 oz) celery, diced
50 g (2 oz) carrot, diced
2 bay leaves
4 tbsp butter

3 tbsp plain flour
475 ml (16 fl oz) double cream
100 ml (4 fl oz) dry sherry
50 ml (2 fl oz) brandy
sea salt and white pepper, to taste

Preheat oven to 200°C (400°F/Gas mark 6). Extract the lobster meat, chop and set aside. Place the lobster shells in a roasting pan with the onion, celery, carrot, bay leaves and butter. Roast in the oven, stirring occasionally, for 45 minutes or until the lobster shells and vegetables have browned. Remove from the oven and strain off the butter into a heavy saucepan. Place the remaining contents of the roasting pan in a large pot. Add 2½ litres (4 pints) and boil until the liquid is reduced by half, about 20 minutes. Strain the stock and discard the solids.

Heat the butter in the saucepan over medium heat. Whisk in the flour and cook the roux for 2 minutes, stirring constantly, until the roux has a nutty aroma. Whisk in the lobster stock and blend well. Then add the cream, sherry and brandy. Simmer for 30 minutes. Season to taste with salt and white pepper. Strain the bisque and stir in the lobster meat until warmed through. Serve hot.

Serves 4

thai lemongrass prawn soup

see variations page 93

Known as tom yum goong, this popular soup gets its sour flavour from both the lemongrass and kaffir lime leaves. Both ingredients – plus fresh galangal and tamarind paste – are available at better grocery stores or Asian markets and can be frozen for future use.

1½ L (2½ pt) water
2 (20-cm/8-in) lemongrass stalks, root end trimmed, smashed with side of chef's knife, and cut into 2½-cm (1-in) pieces
3 slices fresh galangal, smashed with side of chef's knife
3–4 fresh or frozen kaffir lime leaves
1 tbsp tamarind paste
1 tbsp bottled Asian fish sauce (nam pla)

12 small Thai chillies or 2 jalapeños, trimmed, deseeded, and thinly sliced on diagonal
2 green onions, thinly sliced on diagonal
2 tbsp roasted chilli paste (nam prik pao) or tom yum paste
325 g (12 oz) raw prawns, peeled and deveined
juice of 1 lime
fresh coriander sprigs, to garnish

Bring the water to the boil in a large saucepan. Add the lemongrass, galangal, kaffir lime leaves and tamarind paste. Bring to the boil and stir in the fish sauce, chillies, onions, roasted chilli paste and prawns. Cover and simmer for 5 minutes or until the prawns are pink and opaque. Remove from the heat and stir in the lime juice. Serve hot, garnished with coriander.

Serves 4

chinese seafood soup

see variations page 94

Chopsticks or spoon? You'll need both for this hearty, flavourful soup.

1 tsp canola oil
4 cloves garlic, finely chopped
340 g (12 oz) thinly sliced Chinese or
    napa cabbage
1 small red Thai or serrano chilli, deseeded and
    thinly sliced on diagonal
1½ L (2½ pt) chicken stock

3 tbsp soya sauce
2 tbsp unseasoned rice wine vinegar
225 g (8 oz) Chinese wheat noodles or linguine
175 g (6 oz) small raw prawns, peeled
    and deveined
275 g (6 oz) bay scallops
4 green onions, thinly sliced, to garnish

In a large saucepan, heat the oil over medium-high heat, and sauté the garlic, cabbage and chilli until the cabbage has wilted, about 2 minutes. Stir in the chicken stock, soya sauce and rice vinegar. Bring to the boil and add the noodles. Cook, covered, until the noodles are almost tender, for about 2 minutes. Add the prawns and scallops, cover and simmer for 2–3 minutes or until the prawns are pink and opaque and the scallops are white and opaque. Serve the soup garnished with green onions.

Serves 4

kerala fish curry

see variations page 95

The cuisine of Kerala, on the Malabar coast of southeastern India, combines subtropical foods with spices brought by Arab traders long ago. Known as fish aviyal, this easy curry is most aromatic served with Coconut Rice (page 270).

¹/₂ tsp tamarind concentrate dissolved in 2 tbsp hot water	175 g (6 fl oz) water
175 g (6 oz) dessicated (not sweetened, flaked) coconut	100 ml (4 fl oz) tinned coconut milk
50 g (2 oz) finely chopped onion	1 serrano or Thai green chilli, deseeded and split lengthwise
1 tsp ground cumin	450 g (1 lb) pomfret, flounder, sole or snapper fillets, rinsed and patted dry, and cut into 5-cm (2-in) pieces
¹/₄ tsp ground coriander	10 curry leaves or 4 bay leaves
¹/₄ tsp ground red pepper	1 tbsp vegetable oil
¹/₄ tsp ground turmeric	
1¹/₂ tsp fine sea salt	

In a food processor, blend the tamarind water, coconut, onion, cumin, coriander, red pepper, turmeric, salt, water and coconut milk until somewhat smooth. Transfer coconut mixture to a large, deep frying pan with a lid. Place the split chilli in the centre and heat to a simmer. Add the fish pieces in one layer, cover and simmer for 10 minutes or until the fish is opaque. Add curry leaves and oil. Simmer for 1 minute more and serve.

Serves 8

oyster stew

see variations page 96

For many families, oyster stew is a dish served on a meatless Christmas Eve or other holiday. For the best flavour and texture, gently simmer the oysters for only a few minutes, so they do not become too tough.

225 g (8 oz) finely chopped leeks
225 g (8 oz) finely chopped onions
2 tbsp butter
5 dozen shucked oysters, liquid reserved
1 L (2 pt) chicken stock

1 bay leaf
$\frac{1}{2}$ tsp dried summer savory
450 g (1 lb) peeled and diced baking potatoes
900 ml (1$\frac{1}{2}$ pt) double cream
snipped fresh chives, to garnish

In a large saucepan, sauté the leeks and onions in butter until transparent, for about 4 minutes. Stir in the reserved oyster liquid, chicken stock, bay leaf, summer savory and potatoes. Bring to the boil and cook until the potatoes are tender, about 15 minutes. Purée the soup in batches, and return to the pan. Stir in the cream and bring to the boil. Reduce the heat, add the shucked oysters, cover and simmer for 4 minutes or until the oysters are just firm. Serve garnished with snipped chives.

Serves 6–8

red snapper veracruzano

see variations page 97

This Mexican classic from the Gulf of Mexico gets its distinctive flavour from both fresh and brined ingredients. Another plus – it's ready in minutes and perfect with a chilled Mexican beer.

2 tbsp canola oil
1 large onion, thinly sliced
4 garlic cloves, minced
2 tbsp chopped pickled jalapeños
3 plum tomatoes, deseeded and chopped
225 ml (8 fl oz) water

100 g (4oz) pimento-stuffed green
  olives, chopped
1 tbsp fresh or 1 tsp dried oregano
4 (175-g/6-oz) red snapper, mahi mahi, tilapia
  or halibut fillets, rinsed and patted dry
coarse sea salt and ground black pepper
lime wedges, to garnish

Heat the oil in a large frying pan over medium-high heat and sauté the onion until golden, about 4–6 minutes. Stir in the garlic and jalapeños and cook for another minute. Add tomatoes and water and cook, stirring, until almost evaporated, about 6–8 minutes. Stir in the olives and oregano. Arrange the fish over the vegetables, cover and simmer for 7 minutes or until the fish is opaque. Season to taste and serve garnished with lime wedges.

Serves 4

seafood zarzuela

see variations page 98

In Mexico, 'zarzuela' means a three-act operetta that alternates between singing and speaking parts. It has given its name to this delicious, three-step dish that features fish and shellfish from both the Gulf and Pacific Coasts of Mexico.

100 ml (4 fl oz) vegetable oil
225 g (8 oz) chopped onions
50 g (2 oz) chopped fresh Italian parsley
225 g (8 oz) long- or short-grain rice
1 (450-g/1-lb) tin chopped tomatoes
    with liquid
225 ml (8 fl oz) bottled clam juice
225 ml (8 fl oz) water

25 g (1 oz) chopped fresh coriander
450 g (1 lb) halibut, grouper or monkfish
    fillets, rinsed and patted dry, cut into
    2½-cm (1-in) pieces
225 g (8 oz) small bay scallops
225 g (8 oz) raw large prawns, peeled and
    deveined
fresh avocado and lime wedges, to garnish

Heat the oil in a large saucepan over medium-high heat. Sauté the onions, stirring, until transparent, for about 5 minutes. Stir in the parsley and rice and cook, stirring, until the rice begins to brown. Stir in the tomatoes, clam juice and water. Bring to the boil, then reduce the heat, cover and simmer for 15 minutes. Reduce the heat to low and stir in the coriander, fish, scallops and prawns. Cover and cook for 10 minutes or until fish and shellfish are opaque. Serve in bowls, garnished with avocado and lime wedges.

Serves 4

singaporean laksa

see variations page 99

A fusion of Chinese and Malay cuisine, this spicy rice noodle soup is a popular street food in Indonesia and China. 'Laksa,' a word meaning 10,000, indicates that the flavouring base has lots of different parts. There are many varieties of laksas, but all are based on noodles cooked in a spicy broth, and are rich and creamy.

for the laksa paste
2 tbsp vegetable oil
$^1/_2$ tsp ground turmeric
$2^1/_2$ cm/1 in fresh root ginger, grated
1 lemongrass stalk, root end trimmed, mashed
    with the flat end of a chef's knife and cut
    into $2^1/_2$-cm (1-in) pieces
3 garlic cloves, minced
2 small Thai or serrano chillies, deseeded
    and chopped
2 tbsp vegetable oil
12 raw jumbo prawns or large tiger or king
    prawns, peeled, shells and heads reserved

900 ml ($1^1/_2$ pt) water
100 ml (4 fl oz) dry white wine
225 g (8 oz) finely chopped onions
2 kaffir lime leaves, fresh or frozen
450 ml (16 fl oz) chicken or fish stock
1 tbsp soya sauce
325 g (12 oz) fine dry rice noodles or vermicelli,
    cooked according to package directions
2 dozen fresh mussels, scrubbed and debearded
chopped fresh coriander leaves and green
    onions, to garnish

Purée the laksa ingredients together in a food processor or mortar and pestle until smooth. For the soup, heat 2 tablespoons oil in a large saucepan and sauté the prawn shells and heads until bright pink. Add the water and wine and bring to the boil. Cook until reduced by half, about 8 minutes. Strain and reserve the stock; discard the solids. Heat 2 more tablespoons oil in the pan and sauté the onions until transparent, about 4 minutes.

Stir in the laksa paste until well blended. Add the reserved prawn stock, kaffir lime leaves, chicken or fish stock and soya sauce. Bring to the boil. Add the cooked noodles and mussels, cover and simmer for 1 minute. Add the prawns, cover and simmer for 2–3 minutes or until the prawns are pink and opaque and the mussels have opened. Serve in bowls, garnished with coriander and green onions.

Serves 6

variations

provençal fish soup with rouille

see base recipe page 75

provençal fish soup marseillaise
Prepare basic recipe. To serve, ladle broth into bowls and serve with toasted bread and rouille. Arrange cooked fish, shellfish and vegetables on platter as a second course with Aïoli (page 262).

cap d'antibes-style fish soup
Prepare basic recipe, adding an extra 225 g (8 oz) chopped bulb fennel and 450 g (1 lb) small new potatoes to the vegetables.

parisian-style fish soup
Prepare basic recipe, omitting shellfish and adding an extra 450 g (1 lb) fish and 1 bay leaf. When fish and vegetables are cooked, pass soup, in batches, through a food mill. Discard solids. Return brothy purée to the pan, bring to the boil, then strain through a sieve. Serve with toasted bread and rouille.

new orleans-style fish soup
Prepare basic recipe, adding 225 g (8 oz) chopped celery to the onions and garlic. Use redfish or red snapper for the fish and prawns for the shellfish. Add 2 teaspoons filé powder or 1 bay leaf and 225 ml (8 fl oz) dry white wine to the water.

clam chowder

see base recipe page 76

manhattan-style clam chowder
Prepare the basic recipe, omitting the flour and cream. Add 1 (400-g/14oz) tin chopped tomatoes with their juice to the clam juices and proceed with the recipe.

mussel chowder
Prepare the basic recipe, omitting the clams and clam juice and using 1 slice more of minced bacon. While the vegetables and cream are simmering, steam 900 g (2 lb) scrubbed mussels in 450 ml (16 fl oz) wine until shells open. Remove the mussels from their shells, strain the cooking liquid through a paper towel and add the mussels and strained liquid to the pan. Proceed with the recipe.

chaudrée
Prepare the basic recipe, using 450 g (1 lb) fresh squid – body only, cut into fine strips – in place of clams, omitting clam juice and adding 450 ml (16 fl oz) dry white wine to the cooking liquid. Proceed with the recipe and cook until squid are opaque.

clam & corn chowder
Prepare the basic recipe, adding 225 g (8 oz) yellow kernel corn with the potatoes. Garnish with chopped Italian parsley.

variations

classic lobster bisque

see base recipe page 79

quick lobster bisque
Instead of basic recipe, thaw and chop 225–450 g (½–1 lb) frozen lobster meat. Mix with the sherry and brandy. Heat 900 ml (1½ pt) tinned or frozen lobster bisque, stir in the marinated lobster and serve hot.

easy lobster bisque
Eliminate roasting and boiling steps. Begin with 225–450 g (½–1 lb) frozen lobster meat, thawed and chopped. Mix with the sherry and brandy; set aside. Heat 900 ml (1½ pt) prepared Alfredo sauce in a large saucepan. Add the lobster mixture and heat through. Purée if you wish and serve hot.

crab & prawn bisque
Follow steps for Easy Lobster Bisque above, using 450 g (1 lb) cooked prawns and 225 g (8 oz) cooked crabmeat in place of lobster.

cold lobster bisque
Prepare the basic recipe. Leave to cool, then cover and refrigerate. To serve, garnish each cup with a swirl of cream and a sprinkling of chopped fresh tarragon.

variations

thai lemongrass prawn soup

see base recipe page 80

thai lemongrass fish soup
Prepare the basic recipe, using 325 g (12 oz) raw fish fillets, cut into 5-cm (2-in) pieces, in place of prawns.

easy thai lemongrass prawn soup
Instead of basic recipe, bring 1½ L (2½ pt) water to the boil. Stir in 2 tablespoons green curry paste; 2 tablespoons fish sauce; 3 green onions sliced on the diagonal; 12 small Thai chillies or 2 jalapeños, deseeded and thinly sliced on diagonal; and 325 g (12 oz) peeled and deveined prawns. Bring to the boil, then reduce the heat and simmer until the prawns are pink and opaque. Stir in the juice of 1 fresh lime and garnish with coriander.

thai lemongrass scallop soup
Prepare the basic recipe, using 325 g (12 oz) bay scallops in place of prawns.

indonesian prawn & chilli soup
Prepare the basic recipe, using 50 g (2 oz) sambal oelek in place of roasted chilli paste. Garnish with lime, chopped coriander and toasted peanuts.

variations

chinese seafood soup

see base recipe page 82

chinese fish soup
Prepare the basic recipe, using 325 g (12 oz) fresh fish fillet, cut into 5-cm (2-in) pieces, in place of prawns and scallops. Simmer the fish for 2–3 minutes or until opaque and firm.

japanese fish soup
Prepare the basic recipe, using 700 ml (1¼ pt) dashi soup stock and 3 tablespoons miso paste in place of the chicken stock and soya sauce.

easy asian fish soup
Prepare the basic recipe, using 900 ml (1½ pt) prepared Asian-style prawn stock (made from 2 prawn-style ramen noodle packages; omit noodles) in place of the chicken stock, soya sauce and wine vinegar.

aussie-style seafood soup
Prepare the basic recipe, using Australian banana prawns for the prawns and Tasmanian blue mussels for the scallops.

variations

kerala fish curry

see base recipe page 83

kerala prawn curry
Prepare the basic recipe, using 900 g (2 lb) large raw prawns, peeled and deveined, in place of fish.

prawn vindaloo
Instead of the basic recipe, simmer 900 g (2 lb) large raw prawns, peeled and deveined, in 700 ml (1¼ pt) prepared vindaloo sauce until pink and opaque. Serve over rice or with naan.

fish molee
Instead of the basic recipe, fry 450 g (1 lb) sliced onion in 1 tablespoon oil until medium brown in a large, deep frying pan with a lid. Add 2 cloves minced garlic, 1 teaspoon grated fresh root ginger, 1 tablespoon ground coriander, ½ teaspoon ground cumin, ½ teaspoon ground turmeric and ⅛ teaspoon ground red pepper. Stir in 50 ml (2 fl oz) water, 225 ml (8 fl oz) coconut milk and 1 tablespoon white vinegar. Bring to the boil, then simmer. Add 450 g (1 lb) boneless fish cut in 5-cm (2-in) pieces, cover and simmer until opaque.

kerala salmon curry
Prepare the basic recipe, using salmon in place of white fish.

variations

oyster stew

see base recipe page 84

oyster & sausage stew
Prepare the basic recipe, adding 225 g (8 oz) fresh pork sausage or chorizo to the leeks and onions.

belgian mussel stew
Instead of the basic recipe, sauté 100 g (4 oz) chopped onions, 100 g (4 oz) chopped carrots and 100 g (4 oz) chopped celery in 4 tablespoons butter until transparent. Whisk in 475 ml (16 fl oz) whipping cream and set aside. Steam 900 g (2 lb) scrubbed and debearded mussels in 475 ml (16 fl oz) dry white wine, covered, until mussels open, about 5 minutes. Strain mussel cooking liquid through muslin, reserving mussels, and whisk into cream mixture. Add mussels, season with salt and ground white pepper and garnish with chopped fresh Italian parsley.

vichyssoise-style oyster stew
Prepare the basic recipe, adding an extra 900 g (2 lb) diced potatoes.

easy oyster stew
Instead of the basic recipe, prepare tinned potato soup according to directions, adding half dry white wine and half double cream in place of stock. Bring to the boil, add 5 dozen shucked oysters, cover and cook until the oysters are just firm. Serve garnished with snipped chives.

variations

red snapper veracruzano

see base recipe page 86

easy snapper veracruzano
Prepare the basic recipe, using 450 g (1 lb) prepared tomato salsa in place of tomatoes and oregano.

prawn veracruzano
Prepare the basic recipe, using 325 g (12 oz) peeled and deveined raw prawns in place of snapper. Cover and cook until the prawns are pink and opaque.

red snapper on a bed of mango
Prepare the basic recipe, using 450 g (1 lb) chopped fresh mango in place of tomatoes. Omit the green olives and oregano. Add 1 tablespoon fresh lemon juice, 1 chopped tinned chipotle in adobo sauce and 1 teaspoon fresh lime juice to the mango mixture, then place the fish on top and proceed with the recipe.

creole snapper
Prepare the basic recipe, using drained capers in place of pickled jalapeños and 2 teaspoons creole seasoning in place of oregano.

variations

seafood zarzuela

see base recipe page 87

coriander-saffron zarzuela
Prepare the basic recipe, adding 1 teaspoon saffron threads to the water and using fresh clams or mussels in place of fish. (Do not use any clams or mussels that have opened before cooking and discard any that do not open after cooking.)

zarzuela with squash, tomatoes & saffron
Prepare the basic recipe, adding 1 teaspoon saffron threads to the water and 225 g (8 oz) diced courgette or yellow summer squash with the seafood.

roasted poblano zarzuela
Prepare the basic recipe, adding 225 g (8 oz) roasted, stemmed, deseeded and chopped poblano chilli to the stock after browning the rice.

smoky chipotle zarzuela
Prepare the basic recipe, adding 50 ml (2 fl oz) bottled smoked chipotle sauce with the seafood.

variations

singaporean laksa

see base recipe page 88

coconut laksa
Prepare the basic recipe, using 1 (400-g/14-oz) tin coconut milk in place of chicken stock.

cockle curry laksa
Prepare the basic recipe, using cockles in place of mussels. Serve each bowl with a spoonful of sambal chili paste to taste and chopped fresh coriander.

lobster laksa
Prepare the basic recipe, using 900 g (2 lb) lobster in place of prawns and mussels. Steam the lobsters first, remove the meat and cut it into small pieces, and reserve. Crack the shells, and proceed with the recipe. Add the reserved lobster meat to the soup right before serving.

katong laksa
Prepare the basic recipe, cutting the cooked rice noodles into small pieces before adding them to the soup.

into the frying pan

From beer-battered English fish 'n' chips to the fried catfish of the Mississippi Delta and fritto misto from the Italian coast, frying makes fish and shellfish especially delectable. Fried seafood tastes great served with malt vinegar as well as tartare and jezebel sauces.

flash-fried calamari

see variations page 116

Calamari – small squid – are so easy and quick to fry, it's no wonder they're on restaurant menus around the world. They taste wonderful with almost any kind of dipping sauce, so offer two or three when you entertain.

vegetable oil for frying
450 g (1 lb) small squid, heads removed, bodies
    cut into thin rings, tentacles left whole
100 g (4 oz) plain flour

2 large eggs, beaten
100 g (4 oz) fine dry breadcrumbs
coarse sea salt, to taste
dipping sauces of your choice

Heat 1 cm (½ in) of oil in a large frying pan over medium-high heat. Rinse the calamari under cold, running water and gently pat dry. Put the flour in one bowl, the beaten eggs in a second bowl and the breadcrumbs in a third bowl.

Toss the calamari with the flour first, then dip the calamari in the eggs and finally in the breadcrumbs. When the oil is hot (test it with a small piece of bread or a thermometer; it should be 190°C/375°F), fry the calamari, in batches, until golden brown. Drain on paper towels and season to taste. Serve hot with dipping sauces.

Serves 4

whitefish beignets

see variations page 117

As an appetiser with a dipping sauce, as a main course with malt vinegar or as a sandwich filling, these crispy, tender nuggets of fish please young and old alike.

vegetable oil for frying
450 g (1 lb) whitefish fillets, rinsed and patted
    dry, cut into 10-cm (4-in) pieces
100 g (4 oz) plain flour

1 tbsp Cajun or Creole seasoning or
    barbecue seasoning
225 ml (8 fl oz) beer
2 large egg whites
coarse sea salt

Heat 1 cm (½ in) of oil in a frying pan set over medium-high heat. Rinse the fish under cold running water and pat dry. In a bowl, whisk together the flour, seasoning, beer and egg whites into a batter. When the oil is hot (test it with a small piece of bread or a thermometer; it should be 190°C/375°F), dip the fish pieces in the batter, then fry in the hot oil, in batches, turning once. When golden brown, remove from the oil, drain on paper towels and add salt, to taste. Serve hot.

Serves 4

crab cakes

see variations page 118

The most succulent crab cakes start with lump crabmeat, which is crabmeat in bigger pieces. Serve these with your favourite dipping sauce for appetisers, a light lunch or atop a salad.

225 g (8 oz) fresh lump crabmeat
75 g (3 oz) fresh breadcrumbs
50 g (2 oz) sliced green onion
1 tbsp Dijon mustard
$\frac{1}{2}$ tsp dried tarragon

$\frac{1}{4}$ tsp dried red pepper flakes
1 large egg, beaten
vegetable oil for frying

Combine the crabmeat, breadcrumbs, onion, mustard, tarragon, red pepper flakes and egg. Shape into eight 1-cm-/$\frac{1}{2}$-in-thick patties. Chill in the refrigerator for about 30 minutes to firm up. Heat 1 cm ($\frac{1}{2}$ in) of oil in a large frying pan over medium-high heat. When the oil is hot (test it with a small piece of bread or a thermometer; it should be 190°C/375°F), fry the crab cakes, in batches, until golden brown, turning once. Drain on paper towels and add salt, to taste. Serve hot.

Serves 4

coconut prawns & jezebel sauce

see variations page 119

Add a little coconut to the batter and you've got a crunchy, exotic, crowd-pleasing appetiser like this one, adapted from a recipe by Paul Prudhomme. These disappear fast, so make more than you think you'll need.

for the jezebel sauce
1 (275-g/10-oz) jar orange marmalade
5 tbsp brown mustard
5 tbsp prepared horseradish

for the prawns
1 tbsp ground red pepper
1 tsp fine sea salt
1½ tsp Hungarian paprika
1½ tsp ground black pepper
1½ tsp garlic powder
¾ tsp onion powder

¾ tsp ground dried thyme
¾ tsp dried oregano
200 g (7 oz) plain flour
1 tbsp baking powder
2 large eggs, beaten
175 ml (6 fl oz) beer
325 g (12 oz) desiccated (not sweetened, flaked) coconut
vegetable oil for deep-frying
4 dozen large, peeled and deveined raw prawns, tails on, rinsed and patted dry

Stir the Jezebel Sauce ingredients together in a bowl; set aside. Combine the seasonings, flour and baking powder in a bowl, then transfer half to a second bowl. Stir the eggs and beer into the second bowl to make a batter. Place the coconut in a third bowl. Heat the oil to a depth of 10 cm (4 in) in a large saucepan or deep frying pan set over medium-high heat. When the oil is hot (190°C/375°F), dredge the prawns, in batches, in the flour mixture, then dip in the batter, then roll in the coconut. Fry in hot oil until golden. Drain on paper towels and serve with Jezebel Sauce.

Serves 12

beer-battered fish 'n' chips

see variations page 120

A classic dish from the British Isles dating back to Victorian times, this uses tender, white-fleshed fish, such as cod, plaice, haddock, turbot, pike, grouper, John Dory or perch.

for the beer batter
100 g (4 oz) plain flour
1 tsp fine sea salt
1 tsp Hungarian paprika
1 tsp ground fennel seed
1 tsp ground white pepper
475 ml (16 fl oz) beer

vegetable oil for deep-frying
100 g (4 oz) plain flour
900 g (2 lb) fresh white-fleshed fish fillets,
    rinsed and patted dry
4 large baking potatoes, peeled, and cut into 8
    wedges each
malt vinegar and Classic Tartare Sauce
    (page 275) to serve

Pour oil to a depth of 7½ cm (3 in) in a deep frying pan or deep-fryer. Heat oil to 190°C (375°F). In a bowl, whisk the beer batter ingredients together until smooth and the batter just coats the back of a spoon. Place 100 g (4 oz) flour on a plate. Dredge the fish in the flour and then in the batter, letting any excess batter drip off. Fry, in batches, until golden brown, about 4 minutes. Drain on paper towels and add salt, to taste. Fry the potatoes, in batches, until golden brown, about 5 minutes. Drain on paper towels and add salt, to taste, and serve with the fish, along with malt vinegar and Tartare Sauce.

Serves 4

cornmeal-fried catfish

see variations page 121

Along the southern Mississippi River, farmers have carved out catfish ponds in the heavy, clay soil. Farm-raised catfish has a cleaner flavour than river-caught. It also tastes great in this classic dish from the American South, usually served with cornmeal fritters known as hush puppies.

vegetable oil for frying
100 g (4 oz) yellow cornmeal
1 tsp ground red pepper
1 tsp fine sea salt
$^1/_2$ tsp Hungarian paprika
$^1/_2$ tsp ground black pepper

$^1/_2$ tsp garlic powder
$^1/_4$ tsp onion powder
$^1/_4$ tsp ground dried thyme
$^1/_4$ tsp dried oregano
900 g (2 lb) farm-raised catfish fillets, rinsed
    and patted dry

Heat 1 cm ($^1/_2$ in) of oil to 190°C (375°F) in a large frying pan. Combine the cornmeal and seasonings in a shallow bowl. Dredge the fish in the cornmeal mixture. When the oil is hot, fry the fish, turning once, until golden brown. Drain on paper towels and season to taste.

Serves 4

fritto misto with salsa verde

see variations page 122

Italian seafood fritto misto, usually served with the green sauce known as salsa verde, often features small whole fish known as whitebait or smelts, prawns, calamari and small sole. The batter is light and eggy, so serve with a fresh squeeze of lemon as well.

olive oil for frying
100 g (4 oz) plain flour
1 tsp salt
1 tsp ground white pepper
4 large eggs, beaten
225 g (8 oz) fresh whitebait or smelts,
    left whole
450 g (1 lb) raw large prawns, peeled and
    deveined, tails on, rinsed and patted dry

450 g (1 lb) small squid, heads removed,
    rinsed and patted dry, body cut into rings
    and tentacles
6 very small sole, cleaned and heads removed,
    rinsed and patted dry
Salsa Verde (page 38) and lemon wedges,
    to serve

Heat 1 cm (½ in) of olive oil to 190°C (375°F) in a large frying pan set over medium-high heat. Combine the flour and seasonings in a shallow bowl. Put the beaten eggs in a second bowl. Dredge the seafood in the flour mixture, then in the beaten eggs. When the oil is hot, fry the seafood, in batches, turning once, until golden brown. Drain on paper towels. Serve with the salsa and wedges of lemon.

Serves 6–8

sautéed sole with browned butter hollandaise

see variations page 123

Sweet, delicate fish meets deep, rich sauce in a taste marriage made in heaven. Smaller lemon sole, tilapia, turbot or flounder fillets work best because they're flat and sauté quickly. For larger Dover sole or any fish fillet that won't fit in a sauté pan, grilling is the better option.

4 (175-g/6-oz) lemon sole, tilapia, turbot
   or flounder fillets
1 tbsp butter
fine sea salt and ground black pepper, to taste

fresh lemon wedges and minced Italian parsley,
   to garnish
Browned Butter Hollandaise (page 276),
   to serve

Rinse the fish under cold, running water and pat completely dry. Heat the butter in a heavy frying pan over medium-high heat. When the butter starts to brown, add the fish and sauté for 4 or 5 minutes, turning once, or until the fish is opaque and lightly browned. Season to taste, garnish with lemon wedges and a sprinkle of Italian parsley and serve with Browned Butter Hollandaise.

Serves 4

barbados-style fried fish

see variations page 124

In the waters off Barbados, flying fish zoom out of the water and dive back in – an amazing sight that people in Japan, Vietnam, Indonesia and the Solomon Islands also see. In Barbados, however, flying fish have become a national symbol and a distinctively flavoured dish.

1 small onion, quartered
1 tsp dried thyme
25 g (1 oz) chopped fresh Italian parsley
1 tsp fresh lime juice
8 (175-g/6-oz) flying fish, tilapia, farm-raised
    catfish or sole fillets, rinsed and patted dry

fine sea salt and ground black pepper, to taste
vegetable oil for frying
2 large eggs, beaten
100 g (4 oz) fine dry breadcrumbs
lime wedges, to garnish

In a food processor, combine the onion, thyme, parsley and lime juice. Process to a purée. Season the fish with salt and pepper, to taste, then spread with the purée on the flesh side. Cover and refrigerate for 1 hour.

Heat 1 cm (½ in) of oil to 190°C (375°F) in a large frying pan. When the oil is hot, carefully dip the fillets in the beaten eggs, then carefully roll in the breadcrumbs. Fry, in batches, turning once, until golden brown, about 6 minutes. Serve with lime wedges.

Serves 8

stir-fried red snapper with fragrant orange oil

see variations page 125

Stir-fried fish and vegetables get a final flourish of fragrant orange oil to finish. Serve with Coconut Rice (page 270), if you like.

for the fragrant orange oil
100 ml (4 fl oz) vegetable oil
1 tbsp freshly grated orange zest
2 whole star anise
1 tbsp black peppercorns

450 g (1 lb) red snapper fillet, rinsed and
    patted dry, and cut into 5-cm (2-in) pieces
fine sea salt
1 tbsp vegetable oil
3 green onions, sliced on the diagonal into
    5-cm (2-in) pieces
225 g (8 oz) sliced mushrooms
100 g (4 oz) thinly sliced Chinese or
    napa cabbage

To make the orange oil, heat the ingredients in a small saucepan over medium heat for 10 minutes. Remove from the heat and leave to steep for 30 minutes. Strain, then set aside. The orange oil will keep, covered in the refrigerator, for up to 2 weeks.

Season the fish with salt, to taste. Heat the vegetable oil in a wok or large frying pan over high heat until smoking. Add the green onions, mushrooms and cabbage, and toss with paddles until the vegetables are wilted and browned. Add the fish and cook, stirring, until opaque. Serve each portion drizzled with 1 teaspoon of the orange oil.

Serves 4

variations

flash-fried calamari

see base recipe page 101

flash-fried clam strips
Prepare the basic recipe, using fresh clams cut into thin strips in place of calamari. Serve with Classic Tartare Sauce (page 275).

fried clam roll
Prepare the flash-fried clam strips variation above, serving the clams strips in a hot dog bun. Serve with Baja Slaw (page 266) and Classic Tartare Sauce (page 275).

aussie-style calamari
Instead of the basic recipe, marinate sliced calamari in a mixture of 2 beaten large eggs, 2 minced cloves garlic, 1 tablespoon soya sauce and 1 teaspoon freshly grated root ginger for 1 hour. Keep covered in the refrigerator. Heat 1 cm (½ in) oil in a large frying pan. Remove calamari from marinade and dust with 225 g (8 oz) plain flour. Fry in batches, turning once, until golden brown. Drain on paper towels and season to taste. Serve with sliced cucumber and prepared sweet chilli sauce.

cajun calamari
Prepare the basic recipe, adding 25 g (1 oz) Cajun or barbecue seasoning to the flour.

variations

whitefish beignets

see base recipe page 102

whitefish po' boy sandwich
Prepare the basic recipe. Split and toast 4 hot dog buns. Spread the inside of the rolls with Rémoulade (page 261). Top the bottom roll with shredded lettuce and thinly sliced tomatoes. Arrange the hot whitefish beignets on top of the tomatoes, replace the top bun, and serve.

oyster po' boy sandwich
Prepare the whitefish po'boy sandwich variation above, using shucked oysters in place of whitefish.

whitefish fingers
Prepare the basic recipe, cutting the whitefish into 15-cm- (6-in-) long pieces before dipping and frying.

lemony whitefish beignets
Prepare the basic recipe, using 1 teaspoon freshly grated lemon zest in place of the Cajun seasoning mixture.

prawn beignets
Prepare the basic recipe, using 900 g (2 lb) prawns in place of whitefish fillets.

variations

crab cakes

see base recipe page 105

whitefish cakes
Prepare the basic recipe, using 225 g (8 oz) chopped whitefish or pollock fillets in place of crabmeat.

fresh salmon cakes
Prepare the basic recipe, using 225 g (8 oz) chopped fresh salmon fillets in place of crabmeat. Serve with Rémoulade (page 261).

smoked salmon cakes
Prepare the basic recipe, using 225 g (8 oz) chopped smoked salmon in place of crabmeat. Serve with Easy Aïoli (page 275).

lobster cakes
Prepare the basic recipe, using 225 g (8 oz) chopped steamed lobster in place of crabmeat. Serve with Ancho-Lime Butter (page 257).

variations

coconut prawns & jezebel sauce

see base recipe page 106

coconut oysters with jezebel sauce
Prepare the basic recipe, using 4 dozen shucked small oysters, in place of prawns.

coconut prawn salad
Prepare the basic recipe. Arrange 900 g (2 lb) baby greens on each of 8 plates.
Divide 450 g (1 lb) tinned, drained and chopped hearts of palm; 225 g (8 oz)
sectioned fresh orange; and 225 g (8 oz) sliced green onion among the plates.
Arrange 6 coconut prawns on each salad and drizzle with a double recipe of
Asian Vinaigrette (page 27).

coconut prawns with sweet chilli sauce
Prepare the basic recipe, using prepared sweet chilli sauce for dipping. Garnish with
coriander and toasted peanuts.

variations

beer-battered fish 'n' chips

see base recipe page 108

beer-battered fish 'n' sweet potato fries
Prepare the basic recipe, using sweet potatoes in place of baking potatoes.

sake-battered fish 'n' taro chips
Prepare the basic recipe, using 100 ml (4 fl oz) sake and 325 ml (12 fl oz) water in place of beer and sliced taro root in place of potatoes.

sparkling wine-battered fish with hollandaise
Prepare the basic recipe, using 225 ml (8 fl oz) sparkling wine and 225 ml (8 fl oz) water in place of beer. Omit the potatoes. Serve with steamed spinach and Blender Hollandaise (page 264) instead of malt vinegar and Tartare Sauce.

beer-battered prawns
Prepare the basic recipe, using raw large prawns, peeled and deveined, in place of fish.

variations

cornmeal-fried catfish

see base recipe page 109

cornmeal-fried catfish nuggets
Prepare the basic recipe, using 900 g (2 lb) catfish nuggets or pieces in place
of fillets.

cornmeal-fried catfish with fried green tomatoes
Prepare the basic recipe. Slice 2 large green tomatoes into 1-cm- (1/2-in-)
thick slices. Dredge in the cornmeal mixture and fry, turning once, until
golden brown.

cornmeal-fried perch
Prepare the basic recipe, using 900 g (2 lb) perch fillets in place of catfish.
Serve with Classic Tartare Sauce (page 275).

southern fried tilapia
Prepare the basic recipe, using 50 g (2 oz) yellow cornmeal and 50 g (2 oz)
plain flour in place of all cornmeal. Use tilapia fillets in place of catfish.

variations

fritto misto with salsa verde

see base recipe page 110

shellfish fritto misto with salsa verde
Prepare the basic recipe, using 450 g (1 lb) large prawns, 450 g (1 lb) shucked oysters and 450 g (1 lb) bay scallops in place of the variety of fish and shellfish.

seafood & vegetable fritto misto with salsa verde
Prepare the basic recipe, using 6 trimmed baby artichokes in place of the small sole and 450 g (1 lb) trimmed asparagus in place of the whitebait. Fry the vegetables first, then the seafood.

fritto misto with aïoli
Prepare the basic recipe, serving it with Aïoli (page 262) in place of Salsa Verde.

catch-of-the-day fritto misto with salsa verde
Prepare the basic recipe, using 450 g (1 lb) each of four different varieties of freshwater or ocean fish fillets cut into 10-cm (4-in) pieces each in place of the variety of fish and shellfish.

sautéed sole with browned butter hollandaise

see base recipe page 112

sautéed sole with blood orange sauce
Prepare basic recipe, omitting hollandaise. Remove fish from frying pan and swirl in 4 tablespoons butter until foaming. Whisk in the juice of a small blood orange. Season, pour over the fish and serve.

sautéed sole with lemon-caper sauce
Prepare basic recipe, omitting hollandaise. Remove fish from frying pan and swirl in 4 tablespoons butter until foaming. Whisk in 1–2 teaspoons fresh lemon juice and 1 tablespoon drained capers. Season, pour over the fish and serve.

sautéed sole with mango chipotle sauce
Prepare basic recipe, omitting hollandaise. Remove fish from frying pan. Add 450 g (1 lb) chopped fresh mango to pan and sauté until softened, about 3 minutes. Add 1 tablespoon fresh lemon juice, 1 chopped tinned chipotle in adobo sauce and 1 teaspoon fresh lime juice. Serve on top of fish.

low-fat sole
Spray the inside of a frying pan with cooking spray and heat over a medium-high heat. When the frying pan is hot, sauté the fish. Serve with a fresh salsa in place of hollandaise.

variations

barbados-style fried fish

see base recipe page 113

cartagena-style fried lobster
Instead of basic recipe, remove and chop meat from 4 medium lobster tails; reserve shells. Combine lobster with 2 tablespoons tomato paste, 50 g (2 oz) chopped green onion and 1 tablespoon Worcestershire sauce. Pack mixture into the shells. Carefully dip into 2 beaten eggs, then dredge in 175 g (6 oz) fine dry breadcrumbs. Fry in vegetable oil, turning once, until browned on both sides.

tapas-style hake
Instead of basic recipe, process to smooth paste 1 small onion, ½ green pepper, 2 garlic cloves and 2 tablespoons olive oil. Season 4 hake fillets with salt and pepper, then spread mixture on flesh side of fish. In frying pan on medium-high heat, sauté fish, topping-side down, in 2 tablespoons olive oil for 4 minutes, then turn and sauté other side until fish is opaque, about 3 more minutes.

thai-style fried fish
Prepare basic recipe, spreading fish with 1 tablespoon green curry paste blended with 2 tablespoons coconut milk in place of the thyme mixture.

béarnaise-style fried fish
Prepare basic recipe, using 2 large shallots in place of onion, dried tarragon in place of thyme and tarragon vinegar in place of lime juice.

variations

stir-fried red snapper with fragrant orange oil

see base recipe page 114

stir-fried prawns with fragrant orange oil
Prepare the basic recipe, using raw, large, peeled, and deveined prawns in place of the fish. Cook prawns until they are pink and opaque.

stir-fried red snapper with asian vinaigrette
Prepare the basic recipe, drizzling the cooked fish with Asian Vinaigrette (page 27) in place of orange oil.

stir-fried salmon & mange tout with fragrant orange oil
Prepare the basic recipe, using salmon in place of snapper and fresh mange tout in place of cabbage.

stir-fried scallops with fragrant orange oil
Prepare the basic recipe, using scallops in place of fish. Cook the scallops until they are opaque.

in the oven

Baked seafood dishes run the gourmet gamut from

classic crab dip to buttered-and-breadcrumbed

scallops served in a shell to traditional casseroles

and trendy seafood flatbreads and pizzas.

classic crab dip

see variations page 142

With or without a disco ball and dancing, any great party needs one nibble that is sure to please everyone, and this is it. Serve it with savoury biscuits, small slices of dark rye bread or toasted rounds of French bread.

225 g (8 oz) cream cheese, softened
1 tbsp milk
175–200 g (6–7 oz) flaked, cooked crabmeat
3 tbsp finely chopped onion
$\frac{1}{2}$–1 tsp prepared horseradish

$\frac{1}{2}$ tsp fine sea salt
$\frac{1}{2}$ tsp ground black pepper
6 drops bottled hot pepper sauce
1 tsp Worcestershire sauce

Preheat the oven to 190°C (375°F/Gas mark 5). Combine all ingredients in a bowl until well blended. Spoon the dip into a baking dish. Bake for 15 minutes or until bubbling. Serve hot.

Serves 8

baked scallops en coquille

see variations page 143

Large, clean scallop shells – available at better delicatessens – make perfect 'plates' for this appetiser or first course.

1 garlic clove, minced
3 tbsp fresh lemon juice
2 tbsp finely chopped fresh Italian parsley
2 tbsp olive oil

25 g (1 oz) butter, softened
8 large sea scallops, rinsed and patted dry
50 g (2 oz) fine dry breadcrumbs

Preheat the oven to 220°C (425°F/Gas mark 7). Arrange 8 clean scallop shells or ovenproof ramekins on a baking tray. In a small bowl, combine the garlic, lemon juice, parsley, olive oil and butter until well blended. Place a scallop in each shell or ramekin. Spoon the garlic mixture over each scallop and top each one with 1 tablespoon breadcrumbs. Bake for 10–15 minutes or until bubbling and golden. Serve hot with crusty bread.

Serves 8

lobster purses

see variations page 144

With a glass of bubbly, these rich lobster parcels make any occasion a celebration.

25 g (1 oz) unsalted butter
3 tbsp brandy
2 shallots, finely chopped
2 cloves garlic, minced
1 medium-sized carrot, finely chopped
225 ml (8 fl oz) dry white wine,
    preferably chardonnay

3 tbsp double cream
salt and freshly ground black pepper,
    to taste
1 (450-g/1-lb) package frozen puff
    pastry, thawed
meat from 2 large, cooked lobster tails,
    cut into 6 (1-cm/$\frac{1}{2}$-in) pieces

In a large sauté pan, melt the butter. Add the brandy, light a long match and carefully ignite. Let it burn for about 1 minute, being careful to stand back, then cover with a lid and allow the flames to die out. Add the shallots, garlic and carrot. Cook for 5 or 6 minutes, until tender. Add the white wine, bring to the boil and reduce by half. Add the cream and turn off the heat. Season with salt and pepper.

Preheat the oven to 220°C (425°F/Gas mark 7). Cut the puff pastry sheets into 6 (15-cm/6-in) squares. Line a baking tray with parchment paper. Place 1 piece of lobster in the centre of each square. Spoon about 2 teaspoons of the cream mixture atop the lobster. Bring the corners of each puff pastry square together, moisten with water and pin closed to form a rectangular parcel. Place on the prepared baking tray. Bake the parcels for 20–25 minutes, until light golden brown and crispy. Serve warm.

Serves 6

thai prawn flatbread

see variations page 145

With a cold beer and marinated cucumbers, this flatbread is delicious hot from the oven or at room temperature.

6 tbsp smooth peanut butter
100 g (4 oz) plain yoghurt
2 tsp brown sugar
1½ tsp soya sauce
1 tsp toasted sesame oil
1 tsp hot chilli oil
2 tbsp unseasoned rice wine vinegar

2 cloves garlic, minced
325 g (12 oz) cooked medium prawns, peeled
    and deveined
1 (30-cm/12-in) prebaked pizza crust
100 g (4 oz) finely chopped red pepper
100 g (4 oz) finely chopped green onions
50 g (2 oz) chopped fresh coriander, to garnish

Preheat the oven to 220°C (425°F/Gas mark 7). In a bowl, combine the peanut butter, yoghurt, brown sugar, soya sauce, oils, rice vinegar and garlic until smooth. Fold in the prawns until well coated. Spread the mixture over the pizza crust so that the prawns are in one layer. Top with pepper and green onions. Bake for 12–15 minutes or until the prawns are opaque. Sprinkle with coriander and serve.

Serves 4 as a main course, 8 as an appetiser

lobster quiche

see variations page 146

Rich and toothsome, this elegant quiche makes a fabulous brunch or lunch. Miniature quiches (see variation page 146) make bite-sized appetisers.

1 (23-cm/9-in) deep-dish pie shell
100 g (4 oz) chopped fresh baby spinach
175 g (6 oz) cooked lobster meat, chopped
50 g (2 oz) diced red onion
50 g (2 oz) diced red pepper

225 g (8 oz) shredded Gruyère or Swiss cheese
4 large eggs
325 ml (12 fl oz) whipping or single cream
$\frac{1}{2}$ tsp fine sea salt
$\frac{1}{2}$ tsp freshly ground black pepper

Preheat the oven to 230°C (450°F/Gas mark 8). Prick the pie shell all over with a fork, and prebake for 5 minutes. Remove from oven and reduce the temperature to 175°C (350°F/Gas mark 4).

Arrange the spinach on the bottom of the crust. Top with the lobster, then the red onion and pepper. Scatter the cheese over the top. In a bowl, whisk together the eggs, cream, salt and pepper. Slowly pour the egg mixture over the lobster mixture in the pie shell. Bake for 35–45 minutes or until a knife inserted in the centre comes out clean. Leave to cool for 15 minutes before slicing and serving.

Serves 6–8

baked halibut en papillote

see variations page 147

Baking seafood in parchment paper – along with aromatic herbs and flavourings – is a time-tested method that results in a moist, succulent dish, with little to no clean-up!

4 (40x40-cm/16x16-in) sheets parchment paper or heavy-duty aluminium foil
4 (175-g/6-oz) halibut fillets (or pompano, grouper, bluefish, red snapper, cod or catfish), rinsed and patted dry
225 g (8 oz) sliced fresh mushrooms
450 g (1 lb) tinned plum tomatoes, drained

25 g (1 oz) chopped fresh tarragon
25 g (1 oz) chopped fresh Italian parsley
50 ml (2 fl oz) dry white wine
50 ml (2 fl oz) extra-virgin olive oil
fine sea salt and freshly ground pepper, to taste

Preheat the oven to 230°C (450°F/Gas mark 8). Lay each sheet of parchment paper on a flat surface and place a fish fillet in the middle of each. Top each fillet with sliced mushrooms and tomatoes and a tablespoon each of tarragon, parsley, white wine and olive oil. Season. Fold the papers, crimping the edges closed, to form 4 packets and place on a baking tray. (The recipe can be prepared to this point, wrapped, and refrigerated for up to 1 day, if you wish.)

Bake, seam-side up, for 14–16 minutes. Do not turn. To serve, place a packet on each plate, leave to cool slightly, then open.

Serves 4

brandade de morue with cherry tomatoes

see variations page 148

This traditional comfort food dish from the Mediterranean uses dried salt cod, usually available at Italian grocery stores. Allow 48 hours to soak the salt cod. Serve with French bread.

900 g (2 lb) boneless salt cod
475 ml (16 fl oz) double cream
10 garlic cloves, peeled
450 g (1 lb) baking potatoes, peeled and diced
fine sea salt, to taste

freshly ground white pepper, to taste
450 g (1 lb) cherry tomatoes
50 ml (2 fl oz) extra-virgin olive oil
2 tsp chopped fresh thyme
2 tsp chopped fresh rosemary

Soak the salt cod in cold water for 48 hours and change the water at least 4 times. Then, cut the salt cod into 8 pieces.

Preheat the oven to 200°C (400°F/Gas mark 6). In a saucepan, heat the cream, garlic and salt cod pieces over medium-high heat until the fish is tender, about 8 minutes. Set aside. Place the potatoes in a large pan, cover with water and bring to the boil. Cook until tender, about 15 minutes. Drain and mash the potatoes. Transfer the fish and cream mixture and mashed potatoes to a food processor and pulse to blend. Season. Spoon the mixture into the centre of an oiled 20-cm (8-in) square baking pan. Surround the brandade with the cherry tomatoes. Drizzle with olive oil, sprinkle with fresh herbs and bake until bubbling, about 15 minutes.

Serves 6–8

banana leaf-wrapped barramundi

see variations page 149

Banana leaves, found fresh or frozen at Hispanic or Asian markets, lend a mild herbal flavour to fish while protecting the delicate flesh from the heat. Barramundi, native to Australian waters, are now farm-raised in the United Kingdom.

1 large banana leaf, fresh or frozen and thawed
    (or 1 large paper bag)
1 whole baby barramundi (about 1–1½ kg/
    2–3 lb), cleaned and gutted, rinsed
    and patted dry

olive oil, for brushing
1 tsp lemon pepper
1 tsp fresh lime zest
sea salt and freshly ground black pepper,
    to taste

Preheat the oven to 200°C (400°F/Gas mark 6). For a fresh banana leaf, remove centre core and discard. Run the leaf under hot water until pliable. Pat leaf dry with paper towels and cut in half horizontally; overlap the two pieces so that they will cover the fish. For a frozen and thawed banana leaf, separate sections of the leaf and overlap two sections so that they will cover the fish.

Score the body of the fish with three slashes per side. Brush the fish with oil and season with lemon pepper, lime zest, salt and pepper. Place fish on the banana leaves, fold in the left and right sides and roll it up like a burrito. If using a paper bag, insert the fish and fold the bag to close. Place the fish on a baking tray. Bake for 25 minutes or until the fish is firm and begins to flake when tested with a fork in the thickest part. To serve, carefully peel back the top wrapping and serve the fish on a platter.

Serves 4

prawn & artichoke casserole

see variations page 150

A great dish for entertaining, this can be assembled ahead of time and doubled or tripled to serve a crowd. It has a flavour everyone loves.

225 g (8 oz) mushrooms, sliced
150 g (6 oz) butter
700 g (1½ lb) cooked medium prawns, peeled
    and deveined
10 tinned artichoke hearts, drained and coarsely
    chopped
25 g (1 oz) plain flour

325 ml (12 fl oz) whipping or single cream
100 ml (4 fl oz) dry sherry
1 tbsp Worcestershire sauce
fine sea salt and ground black pepper, to taste
¼ tsp paprika
50 g (2 oz) freshly grated Parmesan

Preheat the oven to 175°C (350°F/Gas mark 4). Sauté the mushrooms in 50 g (2 oz) of the butter until soft. Layer a 3½-L (6-pt) casserole dish with the mushrooms, prawns and artichoke hearts. In a saucepan, melt the remaining butter and whisk in the flour. Cook, whisking, for 3 minutes. Gradually pour in the cream and whisk until the sauce has thickened. Add the sherry, Worcestershire sauce, salt, pepper and paprika. Pour the sauce over the casserole ingredients and top with the Parmesan. Bake for 35–40 minutes or until browned and bubbling.

Serves 8

moroccan baked fish

see variations page 151

A spice caravan of flavour infuses this dish as it bakes. Serve it with a flatbread, such as pita or naan, warmed in the oven, or couscous to soak up all the juices.

1 large onion, thinly sliced
1 large tomato, thinly sliced
1 lemon, ends trimmed and thinly sliced
4 (175–225-g/6–8-oz) fish fillets, such as red
    snapper, ocean perch, haddock or John Dory,
    rinsed and patted dry
1 tbsp ground cumin

1 tbsp sweet Hungarian paprika
1 tbsp ground coriander
1 tsp ground caraway seeds
$1/8$ tsp ground red pepper
fine sea salt
2 tbsp olive oil

Preheat the oven to 190°C (375°F/Gas mark 5). Oil a 33x23-cm (13x9-in) baking dish. Place a layer of onion, then tomato, then lemon in the baking dish. Place the fish fillets on the lemon slices. Combine the cumin, paprika, coriander, caraway, red pepper and salt in a bowl. Sprinkle the spice mixture over the fish, then drizzle with olive oil. Cover and bake for 35 minutes or until the fish begins to flake when tested with a fork in the thickest part.

Serves 4

variations

classic crab dip

see base recipe page 127

classic prawn dip
Prepare the basic recipe, using small tinned prawns, drained, in place of crab.

crab rangoon dip
Instead of the basic recipe, prepare Crab Rangoon (page 69), but bake it according to the Classic Crab Dip recipe. Serve Crab Rangoon Dip with fried wontons.

curried prawn dip
Prepare the basic recipe, using small tinned prawns, drained, in place of crab. Use chopped green onions in place of onion and 1 teaspoon curry powder in place of horseradish and Worcestershire sauce.

crab-stuffed mushrooms
Prepare the basic recipe. Instead of spooning the crab dip into a baking dish, spoon it into 450 g (1 lb) cleaned mushroom caps. Arrange the stuffed mushrooms on a baking tray and bake at 190°C (375°F/Gas mark 5) until bubbling, about 15 minutes.

baked scallops en coquille

see base recipe page 128

bay scallops en coquille
Prepare basic recipe, using 450 g (1 lb) bay scallops in place of sea scallops and bake for just 8–10 minutes.

coquilles st. jacques
Instead of basic recipe, bring 50 ml (2 fl oz) dry white wine, 2 tablespoons fresh lemon juice and 1 teaspoon dried tarragon to the boil. Whisk in 225 ml (8 fl oz) double cream and 2 teaspoons Dijon mustard. Cook, whisking, until mixture thickens. Divide scallops among 8 ramekins. Spoon sauce over each and top with 1 tablespoon fine dry breadcrumbs. Bake at 220°C (425°F/Gas mark 7) for 15 minutes or until bubbling.

archangels on horseback
Instead of the basic recipe, cut 4 slices of bacon in half lengthwise. Wrap 8 scallops in a half strip each and secure with toothpicks. Bake at 220°C (425°F/Gas mark 7) for 12–15 minutes or until bacon has browned and scallops are opaque and firm.

angels on horseback
Prepare Archangels on Horseback variation above, using 8 large shucked oysters in place of scallops.

variations

lobster purses

see base recipe page 131

lobster purses with steamed spinach & browned butter hollandaise
Prepare basic recipe. Serve each lobster parcel on a bed of steamed spinach.
Drizzle Browned Butter Hollandaise (page 276) around the perimeter
of plate.

lobster purses with roasted asparagus & orange hollandaise
Prepare basic recipe. Serve each lobster parcel with roasted asparagus. Drizzle
Orange Hollandaise (page 276) around the perimeter of plate.

lobster beggar's purses
Prepare lobster filling. In place of puff pastry, use 8 crêpes. Spoon hot lobster
filling into the centre of each crêpe and draw up sides to form a pouch. Secure
the top with a blanched blade of fresh chive or a food-safe ribbon.

coquilles st. jacques purses
Prepare Coquille St. Jacques filling (page 143). In place of puff pastry, use
8 crêpes. Spoon hot scallop filling into the centre of each crêpe and draw
up the sides to form a pouch. Secure top with a blanched blade of fresh
chive or a food-safe ribbon.

thai prawn flatbread

see base recipe page 132

thai prawn & chicken flatbread
Prepare basic recipe, using 175 g (6 oz) boneless, skinless chicken breast, cut into
5-cm (2-in) pieces, in place of half the prawns.

coconut green curry prawn flatbread
Prepare basic recipe, using coconut milk in place of yoghurt and 2 teaspoons green
curry paste in place of soya sauce and sesame oil.

artichoke, prawn & red pepper pizza
Instead of basic recipe, combine 325 g (12 oz) medium prawns with 50 ml (2 fl oz)
olive oil, 2 minced cloves garlic, salt and pepper. Arrange 450 g (1 lb) chopped
tinned artichoke hearts and 225 g (8 oz) sliced red pepper on a pizza crust. Spoon
the prawns over and smooth so that they are in one layer. Scatter with 50 g (2 oz)
freshly grated Parmesan and bake at 220°C (425°F/Gas mark 7) for 12–15 minutes.

white clam pizza
Prepare the Artichoke, Prawn & Red Pepper Pizza (above), but in place of prawns,
use 450 g (1 lb) frozen and thawed chopped white clams.

variations

lobster quiche

see base recipe page 134

crab quiche
Prepare the basic recipe, using 175 g (6 oz) jumbo lump crabmeat in place of lobster.

southern-style prawn & bacon quiche
Prepare the basic recipe, using 225 g (8 oz) cooked, peeled, deveined and chopped medium prawns, and 175 g (6 oz) cooked and crumbled bacon in place of lobster. Use grated medium Cheddar in place of Gruyère.

crustless seafood quiche
Prepare the basic recipe, omitting the pie shell. Oil the inside of a 23-cm (9-in) baking dish. Arrange the lobster, vegetables and cheese in the dish. Pour the egg mixture over and bake according to recipe.

miniature lobster quiches
Prepare the basic recipe, using 16–20 prepared, prebaked miniature tartlet shells. Place a piece of lobster in each shell. Divide the vegetables and cheese among the tartlets. Fill each shell with the egg mixture. Bake for 15–20 minutes or until browned and bubbling.

variations

baked halibut en papillote

see base recipe page 135

foil-wrapped halibut on the barbecue
Prepare the basic recipe, using aluminium foil. Prepare a medium-hot fire in your barbecue. Place the foil packages on the barbecue, seam-side up, close the lid, and cook for 14–16 minutes.

sake sea bass on the barbecue
Instead of the basic recipe, use 4 (175-g/6-oz) sea bass fillets in the centre of a piece of aluminium foil. Top each with 2 tablespoons sake, 1 teaspoon soya sauce, ¼ teaspoon freshly grated root ginger, ¼ teaspoon brown sugar and 2 tablespoons chopped green onion. Prepare a medium-hot fire in your barbecue. Place the foil packages on the barbecue, seam-side up, close the lid and cook for 14–16 minutes.

lemon-herb trout en papillote
Prepare the basic recipe, using trout in place of halibut. Omit tomatoes. Add 1 teaspoon fresh lemon juice to each trout before folding the parcels.

salmon en papillote
Prepare the basic recipe, using salmon in place of halibut.

variations

brandade de morue with cherry tomatoes

see base recipe page 136

brandade sandwich
Prepare basic recipe. Cut a French roll in half. Brush cut sides generously with olive oil. Place a lettuce leaf on the bottom, then top with 50 g (2 oz) brandade, 50 g (2 oz) baked cherry tomatoes and the other half of the roll.

brandade-stuffed cherry tomatoes
Prepare basic brandade, drizzle with olive oil and bake until bubbling. Scoop out a little of the flesh of each cherry tomato and cut a small slice off the bottom so it sits firmly. Stuff each tomato with 1 rounded teaspoon brandade, sprinkle with the herbs and arrange on a platter.

brandade-stuffed mushrooms
Prepare basic brandade, omitting cherry tomatoes. Stuff 16 mushroom caps with the mixture, drizzle with olive oil, scatter with the herbs and bake until bubbling.

brandade crostini
Prepare basic brandade, omitting tomatoes. Slice Italian or French bread, brush with olive oil and toast at 175°C (350°F/Gas mark 4) for 15 minutes. Spoon 1 tablespoon brandade on each slice. Drizzle with olive oil, sprinkle with herbs and bake until warmed through.

banana leaf-wrapped barramundi

see base recipe page 138

barbecued banana leaf-wrapped barramundi
Prepare the basic recipe. Prepare an indirect fire in your barbecue (the heat on one side, no heat on the other). Barbecue the leaf-wrapped barramundi over direct heat for 5 minutes on each side until the leaves are smoldering. Transfer the fish to the indirect side, close the lid and cook for another 15 minutes.

barbecued malaysian leaf-wrapped snapper
Prepare the basic recipe, using snapper in place of barramundi and slathering the fish with 50 g (2 oz) prepared chilli paste in place of the lemon pepper, lime zest, salt and pepper. Barbecue as in the variation above.

rainforest leaf-wrapped fish
Prepare the basic recipe, using catfish, trout or other freshwater fillets in place of whole barramundi. Season the fish before wrapping with 50 g (2 oz) prepared achiote paste in place of the lemon pepper, lime zest, salt and pepper.

barbadian leaf-wrapped fish
Prepare the basic recipe, using grouper in place of whole barramundi. Season the fish with fresh thyme in place of lemon pepper.

variations

prawn & artichoke casserole

see base recipe page 139

crab & artichoke casserole
Prepare the basic recipe, using 225 g (8 oz) lump or flaked crabmeat in place of the prawns.

prawn mac & cheese
Prepare the basic recipe, omitting mushrooms, artichokes, sherry and 50 g (2 oz) butter. Mix 450 g (1 lb) cooked macaroni with the prawns in the prepared casserole. Make the basic cream sauce, adding 75 g (3 oz) grated aged sharp Cheddar cheese. Pour the sauce over the macaroni and prawns, top with another 75 g (3 oz) grated Cheddar and bake.

lobster mac & cheese
Prepare the Prawn Mac & Cheese (above), using the cooked and chopped meat of 4 lobster tails in place of prawns.

prawn & artichoke pot pies
Prepare the basic recipe, using 8 oiled ovenproof ramekins instead of the dish. Top each ramekin with a round of puff pastry. Bake at 220°C (425°F/Gas mark 7) until the puff pastry is puffed and golden, about 15–20 minutes.

variations

moroccan baked fish

see base recipe page 140

lebanese baked fish
Prepare the basic recipe, using 1 tablespoon ground sumac, 1 tablespoon ground cumin and 1 teaspoon salt in place of spice mixture. Mix 2 cloves minced garlic with the olive oil and drizzle over fish before baking.

italian baked fish
Prepare the basic recipe, using 25 g (1 oz) dried Italian seasoning in place of seasoning mixture.

french fish gratin
Instead of the basic recipe, arrange 4 fish fillets, such as turbot, haddock or halibut, in one layer in the oiled dish. Pour 100 ml (4 fl oz) dry white wine and 1 tablespoon fresh lemon juice over fish. Cover and bake at 200°C (400°F/Gas mark 6) for 20 minutes. Pour 100 ml (4 fl oz) heavy cream over the fish, sprinkle with 75 g (3 oz) grated Gruyère and bake, uncovered, until browned and bubbling, about 15 more minutes.

french scallop gratin
Prepare French Fish Gratin (above), using 450 g (1 lb) scallops in place of fish. Adjust cooking time accordingly – because of their large surface area, scallops cook quickly.

on the barbecue

A hot fire, a slathering of olive oil and a seasoning or marinade of your choice are all you need to barbecue perfect fish and shellfish. Barbecuing adds a caramelised flavour, plus you have a world of sauces and accompaniments that heighten the colour and texture of each barbecued dish.

barbecued mini tuna 'burgers' with rémoulade

see variations page 168

As a 'little plates' tapas offering, these easy burgers go from barbecue to platter in minutes. Tuna is one fish that tastes best when seared and served rare or when barbecued to medium.

50 ml (2 fl oz) olive oil, plus extra for brushing
2 tbsp tarragon vinegar
1 bay leaf, crumbled
8 small artisanal rolls such as ciabattini,
    sliced in half

8 (75-g/3-oz) tuna steaks, cut 2½ cm (1 in)
    thick, rinsed and patted dry
Rémoulade (page 261), to serve

Prepare a hot fire in your barbecue. In a small bowl, mix together the olive oil, tarragon vinegar and bay leaf. Brush the cut sides of the rolls with more olive oil. Barbecue the tuna steaks for 2½–3 minutes per side for medium-rare (3–4 minutes for medium). Baste with the oil and tarragon mixture several times while barbecuing. Only turn the fish once.

During the last few minutes of barbecuing, place the rolls, cut-sides down, on the barbecue rack, and barbecue until the bread is golden and has good marks. To serve, place a tuna steak in each roll and top with the Rémoulade.

Serves 8

rum & lime-barbecued prawns on the barbie

see variations page 169

Australian slang for a barbecue, the 'barbie' lends a caramelised, slightly smoky flavour to prawns sizzled on it. Shellfish continue to cook for a minute or two after you barbecue them, so pull them off right before you think they're done. To make sure the prawns get evenly cooked, thread them on the skewers without crowding.

6 (30-cm/12-in) bamboo skewers
50 g (2 oz) unsalted butter, melted
2 tbsp freshly squeezed lime juice (from about 2 limes)
2 tbsp dry sherry or rum (white or dark)

2 finely chopped green onions with some of the green
2 tsp freshly grated root ginger
24 raw, large prawns, peeled and deveined, rinsed and patted dry

Soak the bamboo skewers in water for 30 minutes. Prepare a hot fire in your barbecue. In a bowl, whisk together the melted butter, lime juice, sherry or rum, green onions and root ginger. Thread the prawns onto the skewers. Reserve one quarter of the lime mixture; brush the prawns liberally with the rest. Barbecue the skewers for 2–4 minutes per side or until the prawns are firm, opaque and have good barbecue marks. Serve the skewers drizzled with the reserved baste.

Serves 6 as a main course, 12 as an appetiser

beachside barbecued mackerel

see variations page 170

For the best flavour, barbecue and eat oily fish like mackerel, herring, anchovies and sardines as soon after they're caught as possible. A driftwood fire on the beach and a tangy finishing sauce of Dijon mustard, butter and lemon make the most of these delicious fish.

4 (450-g/1-lb) mackerel, dressed, rinsed
  and patted dry
50 g (2 oz) unsalted butter, melted
1 tsp Dijon mustard
1 tsp fresh lemon juice

25 g (1 oz) finely chopped fresh Italian parsley
fine sea salt and freshly ground pepper, to taste
lemon wedges, to garnish

Make 2 or 3 slashes on each side of the fish. Press each mackerel open, like a book. Combine the melted butter, mustard, lemon juice and parsley. Brush the fish, inside and out, with the melted butter mixture, then season to taste.

Prepare a hot fire in your barbecue. Oil a perforated barbecue rack and place the mackerel, still open like a book, skin-side down, on the barbecue rack. Barbecue the fish for 10 minutes or until the flesh flakes easily when tested with a fork in the thickest part. Do not turn. (Mackerel are so thin you don't have to turn them.) Serve garnished with lemon wedges.

Serves 4

campfire trout

see variations page 171

It may not be instant gratification, but close to it when you can barbecue fish you've
just caught. Here's an easy way to do it. You can also use fresh-caught perch, bluegill,
crappie or walleye pike.

4 (325-g/12-oz) whole trout, cleaned, rinsed
    and patted dry
4 tbsp olive oil, plus more for brushing
16 lemon slices, cut 3 mm ($^{1}/_{8}$-in) thick

8 sprigs fresh rosemary
fine sea salt and freshly ground black pepper,
    to taste

Prepare a campfire outdoors or a wood fire in a charcoal barbecue or a fireplace, using
seasoned hardwoods such as oak, maple or hickory. (Do not use pine, as it lends a resin-like
taste and causes flare-ups.) Place each trout, skin-side down, on a flat surface. Drizzle 1
tablespoon olive oil in the cavity of each fish, then place 4 lemon slices and 2 sprigs of
rosemary in the cavity. Brush each trout with more olive oil and season to taste. Place the
fish in two oiled, hinged barbecue baskets. When the coals have turned grey and you have a
medium-hot fire, barbecue the fish in the baskets for 5 minutes on one side, then turn
baskets over and cook the fish on the other side. Keep turning until the fish begins to flake
easily when tested with a fork in the thickest part, but is still moist, about 15 minutes total.

Serves 4

barbecued yabbies with ginger-lime sauce

see variations page 172

Yabbies are Australian freshwater crustaceans, much like crayfish or lobster. Like lobster, you boil or steam them first, then add the flavour of the barbecue. Outside Australia, use jumbo prawns, spot prawns, langoustines or large crayfish.

4 tbsp olive oil, divided, plus more for brushing
juice of 1 lime
25 g (1 oz) chopped fresh coriander leaves
2 tsp freshly grated root ginger
sea salt, to taste

900 g (2 lb) yabbies, jumbo prawns, spot prawns, langoustines or large crayfish, uncooked, shells on, deveined, rinsed and patted dry

Prepare a medium-hot fire in your barbecue. In a bowl, whisk the olive oil, lime juice, coriander and root ginger together. Season to taste. Bring a large pot of salted water to the boil. Add the shellfish and cook until they turn red, about 5 or 6 minutes. Immediately remove the shellfish with tongs, run under cold water and transfer to a cutting board. With a large, sharp knife, remove the tail shells only and discard. Brush shellfish on all sides with olive oil. Place the shellfish on the barbecue, cover and cook for 2 minutes. Turn the shellfish, cover and barbecue again for 2 minutes. Serve drizzled with Ginger-Lime Sauce (page 39).

Serves 6

woo hoo barbecued halibut with papaya salsa

see variations page 173

Woo hoo is right! First you get the hit of hot piri-piri sauce, then the sweetness of the fish, then the cooling salsa. Only marinate the fish for a short time – under 30 minutes – or the tender fish could be 'cooked' by the acid in the marinade and you'll have ceviche instead. Piri-piri is made from hot peppers brought to southern Africa by Portuguese explorers by way of South America.

4 (175-g/6-oz) halibut fillets (or pompano, grouper, bluefish, red snapper, cod or catfish), rinsed and patted dry
1–2 tsp bottled piri-piri or other hot pepper sauce
2 cloves garlic, minced

2 tsp fresh lemon juice
50 ml (2 fl oz) canola oil
sea salt and freshly ground black pepper, to taste
Papaya & Lime Salsa (page 277), to serve

Prepare a hot fire in your barbecue. In a bowl, combine the piri-piri sauce, garlic, lemon juice and canola oil. Season to taste. Brush the marinade over both sides of the fish and leave to marinate for just 30 minutes.

Measure how thick the fish is in the thickest part (it's usually about 2 cm/¾ in). Calculate your barbecuing time based on 4 minutes per centimetre of thickness (about 8 minutes total for a 2-cm-/¾-in-thick fillet). So barbecue the fish for 3½–4 minutes per side, turning once, or until the fish begins to flake when tested with a fork in the thickest part. Serve with the salsa.

Serves 4

baja fish tacos

see variations page 174

Famous in Baja California, these fish tacos have a delicate texture yet a hearty barbecue flavour. Enjoy them with a pitcher of Mexican beer or a frosty margarita.

½ head red cabbage, cored and thinly sliced
2 tbsp white vinegar
salt and ground black pepper, to taste
2 ripe avocados, peeled and pitted
100 ml (4 fl oz) soured cream
2 tbsp fresh lime juice

6 skinless mahi mahi, pompano, yellow snapper, halibut or cod fillets, rinsed and patted dry
vegetable oil
warm flour tortillas, to serve
chopped fresh coriander, to garnish

Combine the red cabbage and vinegar in a medium bowl and season to taste. Purée the avocados, soured cream and lime juice in a food processor or blender; season to taste.

Prepare a hot fire in your barbecue. Brush the fish with oil, then season to taste. Measure how thick the fish is in the thickest part (it's usually about 2 cm/¾ in). Calculate your barbecuing time based on 4 minutes per centimetre of thickness (about 8 minutes total for a 2-cm-/¾-in-thick fillet).

To serve, cut the fish into strips and place in warm tortillas. Garnish with the slaw, avocado cream and coriander.

Serves 6

seared scallops with roasted red pepper & basil purée

see variations page 175

Sweet, meaty scallops continue to cook for at least a minute after you take them off the barbecue, so once they have a good, seared crust, they're basically done. So don't overcook!

1 (325-g/12-oz) jar roasted red
  peppers, drained
50 g (2 oz) unsalted butter, softened
fine sea salt and freshly ground black pepper,
  to taste

20 medium scallops, rinsed and patted dry
olive oil, for brushing
25 g (1 oz) fresh basil leaves, stacked together,
  and cut into chiffonade strips

Prepare a hot fire in your barbecue. Place a cast-iron barbecue griddle or frying pan on the barbecue grate and let it get hot enough that a drop of water sizzles immediately. Place the roasted red peppers and butter in a food processor and process until puréed. Season to taste. Brush the scallops with olive oil and season to taste. Barbecue scallops on the hot griddle or in the hot frying pan for 2 minutes per side or until the scallops are seared and almost opaque. Stir the basil chiffonade into the roasted red pepper puree. Serve the scallops atop the purée.

Serves 4

stir-barbecued salmon with cherry tomatoes & mange tout

see variations page 176

Stir-barbecuing involves marinating foods cut into small pieces, then placing them in a perforated metal barbecue wok over a hot fire. You use wooden paddles or barbecue spatulas to stir-barbecue the food, giving it a great flavour at it cooks. Serve with steamed rice, if you like.

Asian Vinaigrette (page 27) or bottled
    teriyaki sauce
450 g (1 lb) skinless salmon fillet, rinsed and
    patted dry, cut into 5-cm (2-in) pieces

12 cherry tomatoes
225 g (8 oz) fresh mange tout
1/2 red onion, cut into small wedges

Place the vinaigrette in a sealable plastic bag. Add the salmon, tomatoes, mange tout and onion. Seal, toss to blend and refrigerate for 30 minutes. Prepare a hot fire in your barbecue.

Set an oiled barbecue wok on the barbecue rack. Transfer the salmon mixture to the barbecue wok using a slotted spoon. Stir-barbecue the salmon and vegetables for 8 minutes, using long-handled wooden paddles or barbecue spatulas to toss. Close the lid of the barbecue to heat through for another 5 minutes before serving.

Serves 4

barbecued swordfish with tomato-spinach orzo

see variations page 177

Swordfish is one of the few fish that you can still get cut into steaks. It's a meaty, oily fish from the colder, deeper waters of the Atlantic and Mediterranean. Rosemary and garlic really accentuate its flavour and firmer texture.

50 ml (2 fl oz) olive oil
1 tsp dried rosemary
1 clove garlic, minced
fine sea salt and freshly ground black pepper,
    to taste

4 swordfish steaks, cut 2½ cm (1 in) thick,
    rinsed and patted dry
Tomato-Spinach Orzo (page 268), to serve

Combine the olive oil, rosemary, garlic and seasonings in a bowl. Brush all over the swordfish and leave to rest for 30 minutes. Prepare a hot fire in your barbecue. Barbecue the swordfish for 4–5 minutes per side, turning once, or until you have good barbecue marks and the swordfish is firm to the touch. Serve with the orzo.

Serves 4

barbecued mini tuna 'burgers' with rémoulade

see base recipe page 153

mini salmon 'burgers' with rémoulade
Prepare basic recipe, using salmon steaks or small fillets in place of tuna.

tuna burgers with hoisin & pickled ginger
Instead of basic recipe, finely mince 900 g (2 lb) fresh tuna (skin and bones removed) with a sharp knife or pulse in a food processor. Season with 1½ teaspoons salt and 1 teaspoon black pepper. Form 8 patties. Barbecue for 2½–3 minutes per side. Serve on buns with hoisin sauce and pickled ginger.

indoor-barbecued mini tuna 'burgers' with rémoulade
Prepare basic recipe, but barbecue burgers on the hob in a heavy frying pan preheated over high heat for 15 minutes (or until very, very hot).

open-face swordfish burgers with tarragon hollandaise
Prepare basic recipe, using swordfish steaks instead of tuna and Tarragon Hollandaise (page 276) in place of rémoulade. Combine 100 g (4 oz) chopped fresh tomato, 100 g (4 oz) chopped pitted Kalamata olives and 2 tablespoons capers. Top each burger with hollandaise, then with some tomato mixture. Serve open-faced on toasted crusty bread.

rum & lime-barbecued prawns on the barbie

see base recipe page 154

rum & lime-barbecued scallops on the barbie
Prepare the basic recipe, using 24 medium scallops in place of prawns.

chilli-basted indonesian prawns
Instead of the basic recipe, baste the prawns with 50 g (2 oz) prepared chilli-garlic paste before barbecuing. Serve with Mango & Lime Salsa (page 265).

prawn teppanyaki
Instead of the basic recipe, brush the prawns with canola oil before putting them on the barbecue. As they barbecue, baste them with 100 ml (4 fl oz) prepared teriyaki sauce. Serve with barbecued rings of fresh pineapple and fried rice.

balinese prawn satay
Instead of the basic recipe, make Satay Sauce by mixing 2 teaspoons Thai red curry paste, 325 ml (12 fl oz) coconut milk, 100 g (4 oz) chunky peanut butter and 1 teaspoon tamarind paste or freshly squeezed lime juice until smooth. Stir in 25 g (1 oz) finely chopped fresh coriander leaves. Brush the prawns with some of the Satay Sauce before putting them on the barbecue. Serve with sliced cucumber, the remaining Satay Sauce and Coconut Rice (page 270).

variations

beachside barbecued mackerel

see base recipe page 157

beachside barbecued bluefish
Prepare the basic recipe, using small bluefish or bluefish fillets in place
of mackerel.

barbecued sardines marseilles-style
Instead of the basic recipe, use 450 g (1 lb) dressed, fresh sardines in place of
mackerel. Brush the fish all over with olive oil and sprinkle with dried fennel,
salt and pepper. Barbecue according to the recipe, then serve garnished with
lemon wedges.

barbadian pompano
Instead of the basic recipe, use small pompano or pompano fillets in place of
mackerel. Brush the fish all over with olive oil and drizzle with 2 tablespoons
fresh lime juice. Sprinkle with 1 teaspoon dried thyme and salt and pepper, to
taste. Barbecue according to the recipe, then serve garnished with lime wedges.

asian-style amberjack
Instead of the basic recipe, use amberjack fillets in place of mackerel. Brush the
fish all over with prepared teriyaki sauce. Barbecue according to the recipe, then
serve with steamed rice and Asian Vinaigrette (page 27).

variations

campfire trout

see base recipe page 158

frying pan-barbecued trout
Prepare basic recipe, using 2 seasoned cast-iron frying pans in place of barbecue baskets. Drizzle an extra tablespoon of olive oil over exterior of each trout. Place frying pans on a grate over campfire, barbecue or in fireplace and heat until very hot. Add fish and barbecue, turning once, about 15 minutes total.

barbecued bacon-wrapped trout
Instead of basic recipe, put 2 tablespoons chopped green onions inside each fish, season with salt and pepper, wrap in 3 bacon slices, secure with toothpicks and barbecue.

barbecued leaf-wrapped trout
Prepare basic recipe, adding 16 cabbage or romaine lettuce leaves blanched in boiling water for 1 minute or until just wilted, then drained and patted dry. Wrap each fish in 4 leaves and secure with toothpicks before barbecuing.

pancetta-wrapped perch
Instead of basic recipe, season 4 perch inside and out with salt and pepper. Place 3 basil leaves inside each fish, then wrap each fish in 1 or 2 slices pancetta and secure with toothpicks. After barbecuing, serve with Aïoli (page 262).

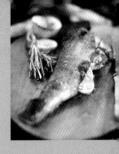

variations

barbecued yabbies with ginger-lime sauce

see base recipe page 160

barbecued yabbies with asian vinaigrette
Prepare the basic recipe, using Asian Vinaigrette (page 27) in place of Ginger-Lime Sauce.

barbecued spot prawns with herbed tomato vinaigrette
Prepare the basic recipe, using spot prawns in place of yabbies and Herbed Tomato Vinaigrette (page 258) in place of Ginger-Lime Sauce.

barbecued yabbie salad
Prepare the basic recipe. Arrange the barbecued yabbies over salad greens and drizzle with the sauce.

barbecued yabbie-stuffed tomato
Prepare the basic recipe, omitting the sauce. Combine 325 g (12 oz) barbecued yabbies with 1 tablespoon Dijon mustard, 100 g (4 oz) mayonnaise, 1 tablespoon fresh dill and salt and white pepper, to taste. Core and hollow out 6 large ripe tomatoes and stuff with the yabbie mixture. Serve chilled.

variations

woo hoo barbecued halibut with papaya salsa

see base recipe page 161

foil-wrapped barbecued woo hoo halibut with papaya salsa
Prepare the basic recipe, wrapping each marinated fillet in aluminium foil.
Prepare a medium-hot fire in your barbecue. Place the foil packages on the
barbecue, seam-side up, close the lid and cook for 14–16 minutes.

woo hoo halibut in parchment parcels with papaya salsa
Prepare the basic recipe, but instead of barbecuing, preheat the oven to
230°C (450°F/Gas mark 8). Place a marinated fillet in the centre of a
40-cm (16-in) parchment paper square. Fold into a parcel and bake for
14–16 minutes.

woo hoo halibut skewers with papaya salsa
Prepare the basic recipe. Soak 12 bamboo skewers in water for 30 minutes.
Cut the marinated fish into 7½-cm (3-in) pieces and thread onto the
skewers, taking care not to crowd the fish. Barbecue for 4 minutes on each
side, turning once.

thai-style barbecued halibut with papaya salsa
Prepare the basic recipe, using 1 tablespoon green curry paste mixed with
50 ml (2 fl oz) coconut milk in place of the marinade.

variations

baja fish tacos

see base recipe page 162

baja prawn tacos
Prepare the basic recipe, using barbecued prawns in place of fish.

baja seared tuna tacos
Prepare the basic recipe, using slices of barbecue-seared tuna in place of fish.

baja swordfish tacos
Prepare the basic recipe, using barbecued swordfish steaks seasoned with smoked paprika in place of fish.

baja lobster tacos
Prepare the basic recipe, using steamed lobster tail meat, cut into pieces, in place of fish.

seared scallops with roasted red bell pepper & basil puree

see base recipe page 164

seared scallops with sweet pea purée
Prepare the basic recipe. In place of the roasted red pepper and basil purée, cook 1 (275-g/10-oz) package frozen petit pois in boiling salted water for 3 minutes or until just tender. Drain, then purée in the food processor with 50 g (2 oz) butter and salt and pepper, to taste.

seared scallops with butternut squash & parmesan purée
Prepare the basic recipe. In place of the roasted red pepper and basil purée, heat 1 (425-g/15-oz) tin butternut squash puree with 25 g (1 oz) freshly grated Parmesan in a saucepan until warmed through and the cheese has melted. Season to taste.

prosciutto-wrapped scallops
Prepare the basic recipe, wrapping each scallop with a strip of prosciutto and securing with a toothpick before barbecuing.

seared monkfish with roasted red pepper & basil purée
Prepare the basic recipe, using 4 monkfish fillets in place of scallops, barbecued for 4 minutes per centimetre of thickness, turning once.

variations

stir-barbecued salmon with cherry tomatoes & mange tout

see base recipe page 165

stir-barbecued prawns with cherry tomatoes & mange tout
Prepare basic recipe, using raw, large, peeled and deveined prawns in place of salmon.

stir-barbecued catfish with corn, cherry tomatoes & courgettes
Prepare basic recipe, using 225 ml (8 fl oz) bottled Italian dressing in place of Asian Vinaigrette, farm-raised catfish fillets in place of salmon and 225 g (8 oz) uncooked corn kernels and 225 g (8 oz) thinly sliced courgettes in place of mange tout.

stir-barbecued prawn satay
Prepare basic recipe, using Satay Sauce (page 169) in place of Asian Vinaigrette, raw peeled and deveined prawns (or jumbo prawns) in place of salmon and 225 g (8 oz) sliced red pepper and 225 g (8 oz) chopped spring onions in place of mange tout and red onion. Garnish with roasted peanuts.

stir-barbecued pacific rim mahi mahi
Prepare basic recipe, using bottled teriyaki sauce in place of Asian Vinaigrette, mahi mahi in place of salmon, 225 g (8 oz) sliced red pepper and 225 g (8 oz) chopped fresh pineapple in place of mange tout and 100 g (4 oz) chopped spring onions in place of red onion.

barbecued swordfish with tomato–spinach orzo

see base recipe page 166

barbecued swordfish with cucumber–dill orzo
Prepare basic recipe, using Cucumber-Dill Orzo (page 279) in place of
Tomato-Spinach Orzo.

rosemary–infused barbecued swordfish with tomato–spinach orzo
Prepare basic recipe, omitting the dried rosemary. Add 2 sprigs of fresh
rosemary to the olive oil, garlic and seasonings in microwave-safe bowl and
cook on high heat for 1 minute. Leave to steep and cool for 15 minutes.
Pour the infused oil over the swordfish steaks and leave to infuse at room
temperature for 30 minutes before barbecuing.

barbecued swordfish with fresh herb butter & tomato–spinach orzo
Prepare basic recipe, topping each barbecued swordfish steak with a pat of
Fresh Herb Butter (page 272) before serving.

marinated barbecued swordfish with tomato–spinach orzo
Instead of the rosemary vinaigrette, whisk together 2 tablespoons fresh
lemon juice, 2 minced cloves garlic, 1 teaspoon sea salt and 50 ml (2 fl oz)
olive oil to make a marinade. Pour the marinade over the swordfish steaks
and marinate at room temperature for 30 minutes. Remove steaks from
marinade and barbecue as in basic recipe.

on a plank

With planked seafood, you get the gentle, aromatic

flavour of the wood quite deliciously different

from the flavour of barbecuing or smoking.

Planking is the simplest way to cook on the

barbecue – just place the plank on the barbecue

and close the lid. Yum!

planked prawns with bistro butter

see variations page 194

In this recipe, the prawns (or jumbo prawns) take on the aromatic wood flavour of the plank while being basted with the Bistro Butter while they cook. You can serve this right from the plank with plenty of crusty bread to mop up the juices.

1 oven plank, soaked in water for at least
   30 minutes
16–24 large raw prawns (or jumbo prawns),
   peeled and deveined, rinsed and patted dry
Bistro Butter (page 272)

While the plank soaks, prepare an indirect fire in your barbecue (with heat on one side, no heat on the other). Arrange the prawns in one layer on the soaked plank, with as much of the prawns touching the wood as possible (for more aromatic wood flavour). Dot the butter over the prawns. Place the plank on the indirect (no heat) side of the barbecue, close the lid and cook for 30–45 minutes, or until the prawns are pink and opaque. Serve immediately.

Serves 4

planked salmon chimichurri

see variations page 195

When you plank a salmon fillet, you don't have to worry about turning it on the barbecue – it's cooked on the plank. Easy! Chimichurri Sauce is a fresh herb vinaigrette from Argentina that really complements salmon. This dish is delicious as a main course – serve it right from the plank if you like – or as an appetiser with barbecued bread, slathered with more Chimichurri.

1 oven plank, soaked in water for at least
    30 minutes
1 skinless salmon fillet, rinsed and patted dry,
    and cut to fit the plank

Chimichurri (page 273)
barbecued bread, to serve

While the plank soaks, prepare an indirect fire in your barbecue (heat on one side, no heat on the other). Place the salmon on the plank. Drizzle the fish with Chimichurri. Place on the indirect (no heat) side of the barbecue, close the lid and cook for 45–60 minutes, or until the salmon begins to flake when tested with a fork in the thickest part. Serve immediately.

Serves 6 as a main course, 12 as an appetiser

macadamia-buttered barramundi

see variations page 196

Get a taste of Australia and New Zealand with this dish. Barramundi are now farm-raised in Britain, or you can substitute Tasmanian ocean trout, Arctic char, hake, haddock or monkfish – all medium-textured fish with great flavour.

for the macadamia butter
100 g (4 oz) finely chopped macadamia nuts
100 g (4 oz) unsalted butter, softened
25 g (1 oz) finely chopped fresh Italian parsley
sea salt and freshly ground black pepper,
    to taste

1 oven plank, soaked in water for at least
    30 minutes
900 g (2 lb) skinless barramundi fillets, rinsed
    and patted dry
lime wedges, to garnish

For the Macadamia Butter, combine the nuts, butter and parsley in a bowl and stir together with a fork. Season to taste.

While the plank soaks, prepare an indirect fire in your barbecue (heat on one side, no heat on the other). Place the barramundi on the soaked plank. Dollop the Macadamia Butter over the fish. Place on the indirect (no heat) side of the barbecue, close the lid and cook for 45–60 minutes, or until the barramundi begins to flake when tested with a fork in the thickest part. Garnish with lime wedges.

Serves 6

alder-planked tilapia with artichoke glaze

see variations page 197

Alder, a hardwood from the Pacific Northwest, adds a gentle woody flavour to the fish. The artichoke glaze, a built-in sauce, adds even more flavour while keeping the fish moist and delicious.

for the artichoke glaze
100 g (4 oz) chopped tinned artichoke
    hearts, drained
225 g (8 oz) mayonnaise
50 g (2 oz) freshly grated Asiago cheese

freshly ground white pepper, to taste
2 alder planks, soaked in water for at least
    30 minutes
4 skinless tilapia fillets, rinsed and patted dry
lime wedges, to garnish

Prepare an indirect fire in your barbecue (heat on one side, no heat on the other). For the Artichoke Glaze, combine the artichokes, mayonnaise and Asiago in a bowl. Stir together with a fork, then season to taste. Place the tilapia on the soaked planks. Spread the glaze over the fish. Place on the indirect (no heat) side of the barbecue, close the lid and cook for 30 minutes, or until the tilapia begins to flake when tested with a fork in the thickest part. Garnish with lime wedges.

Serves 4

planked monkfish tapas

see variations page 198

For a wonderful warm weather party, serve this colourful fish appetiser with toasted bread and a dollop or two of Aïoli (page 262), along with a chilled sangria.

for the topping
100 ml (4 fl oz) olive oil
2 cloves garlic, minced
100 ml (4 fl oz) chopped red pepper
100 ml (4 fl oz) chopped green onion
1 tsp sherry vinegar or fresh lemon juice,
    or to taste

fine sea salt and freshly ground black pepper,
    to taste
2 cedar, oak or maple planks, soaked in water
    for at least 30 minutes
4 skinless monkfish fillets, rinsed and
    patted dry

Prepare an indirect fire in your barbecue (heat on one side, no heat on the other). For the topping, combine the olive oil, garlic, pepper, green onion and sherry vinegar in a food processor. Pulse until very finely chopped. Season to taste.

Place the monkfish on the soaked planks. Spread the topping over the fish. Place on the indirect (no heat) side of the barbecue, close the lid and cook for 45–60 minutes, or until the monkfish begins to flake when tested with a fork in the thickest part. Serve immediately.

Serves 8 as an appetiser

tuna niçoise on a plank

see variations page 199

In this new take on the classic recipe from Nice, all the star ingredients go on the plank, then they are served over fresh greens. Enjoy with a glass of chilled rosé and a crusty baguette.

50 ml (2 fl oz) red wine vinegar
2 tbsp minced shallot
1 tbsp Dijon mustard
1 large clove garlic, minced
1 tsp anchovy paste
175 ml (6 fl oz) extra-virgin olive oil
fine sea salt and freshly ground black pepper,
    to taste
1 oven plank or 2 thin planks, soaked in water
    for at least 30 minutes

4 fresh tuna steaks, cut 2½ cm (1 in) thick,
    rinsed and patted dry
325 g (12 oz) thin green beans or haricots verts,
    fresh or frozen, trimmed
450 g (1 lb) cherry or grape tomatoes
3 large hard-boiled eggs, shelled and quartered
225 g (8 oz) brine- or oil-cured niçoise olives
450 g (1 lb) fresh leafy greens, to serve
1½ tbsp finely chopped fresh basil, to garnish

Prepare an indirect fire in your barbecue (heat on one side, no heat on the other). For the Red Wine Vinaigrette, combine the red wine vinegar, shallot, Dijon mustard, garlic, anchovy paste and olive oil in a bowl and whisk to blend. Season to taste. Place the tuna on the soaked plank(s). Arrange the beans, cherry tomatoes, eggs and olives over the tuna. Drizzle with half of the vinaigrette. Place on the indirect (no heat) side of the barbecue, close the lid and cook for 30 minutes, or until the beans are crisp-tender. Arrange the salad greens on 4 plates and top with the tuna, beans, cherry tomatoes, eggs and olives. Drizzle with the remaining vinaigrette and top with the basil.

Serves 4

planked mahi mahi with fresh pineapple salsa

see variations page 200

Fresh salsas are also delicious as built-in sauces for planked seafood. Just remember to brush the fish or shellfish with olive oil first to help keep them moist and protected from the heat of the barbecue.

2 thin planks, soaked in water for at least
    30 minutes
6 skinless mahi mahi fillets (or pompano, yellow
    snapper, halibut or cod), rinsed and
    patted dry
olive oil, for brushing

salt and ground black pepper, to taste
Pineapple & Lime Salsa (page 277)
warm flour tortillas, to serve
soured cream and chopped fresh coriander,
    to garnish

Prepare an indirect fire in your barbecue (heat on one side, no heat on the other). Brush the mahi mahi with olive oil and season to taste. Place the mahi mahi on the plank(s) and top with the salsa. Place on the indirect (no heat) side of the barbecue, close the lid and cook for 30–45 minutes, or until the fish begins to flake when tested with a fork in the thickest part.

To serve, cut the salsa-topped fish into chunks and place in warm flour tortillas, garnished with soured cream and coriander.

Serves 6

smoke-planked lemon–tarragon snapper

see variations page 201

By adding wood chips to the fire, you can add a smoky flavour to seafood that you plank. Serve this as a main course with Lemon Rice (page 281) or as an appetiser with savoury biscuits.

2 thin planks, soaked in water at least
    30 minutes
handful dry hardwood chips or pellets, such as
    mesquite, hickory or pecan
100 g (4 oz) unsalted butter, softened

25 g (1 oz) snipped fresh tarragon leaves
1 tbsp fresh lemon juice
4 red snapper fillets, rinsed and patted dry
fine sea salt and freshly ground black pepper,
    to taste

Soak the planks while you prepare an indirect fire in your barbecue (heat on one side, no heat on the other). For a gas barbecue, place a handful of dry wood chips in an aluminium foil packet, seal then poke holes in the top for the smoke to escape. Place packet near a burner. For a charcoal barbecue, scatter the wood chips on hot coals.

In a bowl, combine the butter, tarragon and lemon juice. Place the snapper on the planks, spread the Lemon Tarragon Butter over the snapper and season to taste. Place the planks on the indirect (no heat) side of the barbecue. When you see the first wisp of smoke, close the lid and cook for 30–45 minutes, or until the fish begins to flake when tested with a fork in the thickest part.

Serves 4 as a main course, 8 as an appetiser

cedar-planked sole roulade

see variations page 202

Use a very thin fish for this fancier dish, such as sole, flounder or turbot. Spread the fillet with the filling, then roll up, place on the plank and drizzle with the sauce. Your guests will be very impressed!

1 oven plank, soaked in water for at least
    30 minutes
Artichoke Glaze (page 184)

4 thin lemon sole fillets, rinsed and patted dry
Herbed Tomato Vinaigrette (page 258)

Prepare an indirect fire in your barbecue (with heat on one side, no heat on the other). Place the fillets, skin-side up, on a flat surface and spread with the Artichoke Glaze. Starting from the widest end, roll up in a spiral. Place seam-side down on the baking plank and drizzle with half the vinaigrette. Place the plank on the indirect (no heat) side of the barbecue, close the lid and cook for 45 minutes, or until the fish begins to flake when tested with a fork in the centre. Serve immediately with the remaining vinaigrette.

Serves 4

maple-planked cod & new potatoes with onion butter

see variations page 203

Tender white cod and a maple plank – a fresh taste of New England with all the flavour of a beachside supper. The Onion Butter keeps everything moist as it cooks on the plank.

for the onion butter
100 g (4 oz) unsalted butter
100 g (4 oz) chopped green onion
50 ml (2 fl oz) dry white wine
fine sea salt and freshly ground black pepper, to taste
2 thin maple planks, soaked in water for at least 30 minutes

4 (175–225-g/6-8-oz) cod fillets, rinsed and patted dry
450 g (1 lb) new potatoes, scrubbed and quartered
chopped fresh Italian parsley, to garnish

Prepare an indirect fire in your barbecue (heat on one side, no heat on the other). Combine the butter, green onion and wine in a food processor and pulse to blend. Season to taste. Place the cod on the soaked planks, then top with the potatoes. Season to taste. Dollop the butter mixture over the fish and potatoes. Place the planks on the indirect (no heat) side of the barbecue, close the lid and cook for 45 minutes, or until the fish begins to flake when tested with a fork in the centre and the potatoes are tender. Garnish with Italian parsley.

Serves 4

variations

planked prawns with bistro butter

see base recipe page 179

planked scallops with bistro butter
Prepare the basic recipe, using scallops in place of prawns.

planked prawns with satay sauce
Prepare the basic recipe, using Satay Sauce (page 169) in place of Bistro Butter. Garnish with chopped fresh coriander to serve.

planked prawn rémoulade
Prepare the basic recipe, using Rémoulade (page 261) in place of Bistro Butter.

planked asian prawns
Prepare the basic recipe, using Asian Vinaigrette (page 27) or 100 ml (4 fl oz) bottled teriyaki sauce in place of Bistro Butter.

planked salmon chimichurri

see base recipe page 180

planked salmon with tomato vinaigrette
Prepare the basic recipe, using Herbed Tomato Vinaigrette (page 258) in place of Chimichurri.

planked salmon rémoulade
Prepare the basic recipe, using Rémoulade (page 261) in place of Chimichurri.

planked ancho-buttered salmon
Prepare the basic recipe, using dollops of Ancho-Lime Butter (page 257) in place of Chimichurri. Top with 225 g (8 oz) chopped fresh tomato, 50 g (2 oz) chopped fresh coriander and 100 (4 oz) chopped green onion before barbecuing.

planked salmon with mustard dill aïoli
Prepare the basic recipe, replacing Chimichurri with Easy Aïoli (page 275), made with an additional 2 tablespoons Dijon mustard and 1 teaspoon dried dill. Top with fresh dill before barbecuing.

macadamia-buttered barramundi on a plank

see base recipe page 183

pistachio-buttered turbot on a plank
Prepare basic recipe, using skinless turbot fillets in place of barramundi, and roasted, chopped, shelled pistachios in place of macadamia nuts. Plank for 30 minutes or until turbot begins to flake when tested with a fork in the thickest part.

pecan-buttered walleye on a plank
Prepare basic recipe, using skinless walleye or other freshwater fillets in place of barramundi, and toasted chopped pecans in place of macadamias. Plank for 45 minutes or until walleye begins to flake when tested.

coriander-buttered trout on a plank
Prepare basic recipe, using skinless trout or other freshwater fillets in place of barramundi, and 25 g (1 oz) chopped coriander in place of macadamias. Plank for 45 minutes or until trout flakes when tested.

orange-buttered sole on a plank
Prepare basic recipe, using skinless sole fillets in place of barramundi, and 1 teaspoon fresh orange zest and 1 teaspoon dried tarragon in place of macadamias. Plank for 30 minutes or until sole flakes when tested. Garnish with orange slices and tarragon sprigs.

alder-planked tilapia with artichoke glaze

see base recipe page 184

alder-planked tilapia with basil aïoli

Prepare the basic recipe, using Basil Aïoli in place of Artichoke Glaze. Make Easy
Aïoli (page 275) and stir in 25 g (1 oz) chopped fresh basil.

alder-planked tilapia with roasted red pepper glaze

Prepare the basic recipe, using drained and chopped tinned roasted red peppers in
place of artichokes in the glaze.

pesto-planked perch

Prepare the basic recipe, using 50 g (2 oz) prepared pesto in place of Artichoke
Glaze and perch fillets in place of tilapia. Serve with sliced fresh tomatoes.

harissa-planked hake with fresh salsa

Prepare the basic recipe, using 50 g (2 oz) prepared harissa in place of Artichoke
Glaze and hake fillets in place of tilapia. Serve with Mango & Lime Salsa (page 265)
or Papaya & Lime Salsa (page 277) to cool off.

variations

planked monkfish tapa

see base recipe page 186

greek-style planked monkfish
Prepare the basic recipe, using 100 g (4 oz) chopped Kalamata olives in place of red pepper. Add 100 g (4 oz) chopped, deseeded cucumber and 1 teaspoon dried oregano to the topping.

asian-style planked monkfish
Prepare the basic recipe, using 50 g (2 oz) miso paste and 100 g (4 oz) chopped green onion in place of the topping.

provençal-style planked monkfish
Prepare the basic recipe, using 100 g (4 oz) chopped fresh fennel in place of red pepper and fresh lemon juice in place of vinegar. Add 1 teaspoon dried tarragon to the topping.

mexican-style planked monkfish
Prepare the basic recipe, adding 50 g (2 oz) chopped, deseeded jalapeño pepper and 100 g (4 oz) chopped fresh tomato in place of red pepper and fresh lime juice in place of vinegar. Add 1 teaspoon ground cumin and 1 teaspoon dried oregano to the topping.

variations

tuna niçoise on a plank

see base recipe page 187

salmon niçoise on a plank
Prepare basic recipe, using 1 skinless salmon fillet in place of tuna steaks.
Cook for 45 minutes or until the fish flakes easily when tested with a fork in
the thickest part. Cut into 4 pieces to serve.

prawn niçoise on a plank
Prepare basic recipe, using 450 g (1 lb) peeled and deveined large prawns in
place of tuna. Cook for 30 minutes or until they are pink and opaque.

barbecued tuna niçoise
Prepare basic recipe, omitting the plank(s). Prepare a hot fire in the barbecue.
Steam the beans until crisp-tender. Brush the tuna steaks with some of the
vinaigrette and barbecue for 2 minutes per side for rare.

barbecued salmon niçoise
Prepare basic recipe, omitting the plank(s) and using a salmon fillet in place
of tuna steaks. Prepare a hot fire in your barbecue. Steam the beans until
crisp-tender. Brush the salmon with some of the vinaigrette and barbecue
for 3½–4 minutes per side, turning once.

variations

planked mahi mahi with fresh pineapple salsa

see base recipe page 188

planked mahi mahi with fresh papaya salsa
Prepare the basic recipe, using Papaya & Lime Salsa (page 277) in place of Pineapple & Lime Salsa.

planked mahi mahi with fresh mango salsa
Prepare the basic recipe, using Mango & Lime Salsa (page 265) in place of Pineapple & Lime Salsa.

planked prawns with fresh mango salsa
Prepare the basic recipe, using peeled and deveined jumbo prawns in place of mahi mahi and Mango & Lime Salsa (page 265) in place of Pineapple & Lime Salsa. Cook for 30 minutes, or until the prawns are pink and opaque.

planked scallops with fresh honeydew salsa
Prepare the basic recipe, using medium scallops in place of mahi mahi and Honeydew & Lime Salsa (page 277) in place of Pineapple & Lime Salsa. Cook for 30 minutes, or until the scallops are firm and opaque.

smoke-planked lemon–tarragon snapper

see base recipe page 190

planked lemon–tarragon snapper
Prepare the basic recipe, but omit the wood chips.

smoke-planked lemon–tarragon scallops
Prepare the basic recipe, using 900 g (2 lb) medium scallops in place of
snapper. Melt the Lemon-Tarragon Butter, toss the scallops in the mixture
then arrange on the planks. Cook for 30 minutes or until the scallops are
firm and opaque.

smoke-planked lemon–tarragon prawns
Prepare the basic recipe, using 900 g (2 lb) peeled and deveined large prawns
in place of snapper. Melt the Lemon-Tarragon Butter, toss the prawns in the
mixture then arrange on the planks. Cook for 30 minutes or until the prawns
are pink and opaque.

smoke-planked lemon–tarragon salmon
Prepare the basic recipe, using salmon in place of snapper.

variations

cedar-planked sole roulade

see base recipe page 191

mediterranean sole roulade
Prepare the basic recipe, using 50 g (2 oz) prepared pesto in place of the
Artichoke Glaze.

roasted red pepper sole roulade
Prepare the basic recipe, using 50 g (2 oz) Roasted Red Pepper Purée
(page 164) in place of the Artichoke Glaze.

provençal sole roulade
Prepare the basic recipe, using 50 g (2 oz) prepared tapenade in place of the
Artichoke Glaze.

planked sole roulade with basil aïoli
Prepare the basic recipe, using 50 g (2 oz) Basil Aïoli (page 197) in place of the
Artichoke Glaze.

maple-planked cod & new potatoes with onion butter

see base recipe page 192

maple-planked haddock with onion butter
Prepare the basic recipe, using haddock in place of cod.

maple-planked whitefish with three-pepper butter
Prepare the basic recipe, using whitefish in place of cod. Add 50 g (2 oz) each chopped red, green and yellow pepper to the Onion Butter and spread on the fish before planking.

maple-planked orange roughy with lemon-tarragon butter
Prepare the basic recipe, using orange roughy in place of cod and Lemon-Tarragon Butter (page 190) in place of Onion Butter.

maple-planked cod with tapas topping
Prepare the basic recipe, using Tapas Topping (page 186) in place of Onion Butter.

roasted

High heat roasting, like barbecuing over a hot fire, helps seafood cook quickly to a crisp exterior and a moist interior. While you're at it, why not roast a vegetable along with it, then whip up an easy sauce – and you've got dinner.

simple roasted prawns & asparagus

see variations page 220

For an easy dinner or a platter-style appetiser, accompanied by a bowl or two of your favourite dipping sauces, this dish has no peer. For a sauce that goes with both roasted prawns and asparagus, try Basil Aïoli (page 197), Sesame Mayonnaise (page 275), Asian Vinaigrette (page 27) or Satay Sauce (page 169). To snap off the tough end of the asparagus stalks, hold an end of each stalk in your hands and bend until the asparagus spear snaps. Discard the woody end.

450 g (1 lb) asparagus, woody ends snapped off
16–24 large prawns, peeled and deveined
olive oil for tossing

fine sea salt and freshly ground black pepper,
to taste

Preheat the oven to 200°C (400°F/Gas mark 6). Place the asparagus in a large bowl, drizzle with olive oil and toss to coat. Arrange the asparagus in one layer on a baking tray and season to taste. Roast for 10 minutes or until the asparagus is crisp-tender and browned.

Place the prawns in a large bowl, drizzle with olive oil and toss to coat. Arrange the prawns in one layer on a large baking tray and season to taste. Roast for 5–6 minutes or until the prawns are pink and opaque. Arrange the prawns and asparagus on a large platter with a bowl of dipping sauce and serve hot or at room temperature.

Serves 4

oyster pan roast with buttery leeks

see variations page 221

Sip a buttery chardonnay while this dish roasts, then toast the good life. Serve this with crusty bread to mop up all the juices.

100 g (4 oz) unsalted butter, melted
3 large leeks, trimmed, rinsed and thinly sliced
900 g (2 lb) fresh, shucked oysters,
    juices reserved

fine sea salt and coarsely ground black pepper,
    to taste

Preheat the oven to 200°C (400°F/Gas mark 6). Place the butter and leeks in a large baking dish, stir to coat the leeks with butter and roast for 5 minutes. Remove, pour in the reserved oyster juices, stir the leeks again and return to the oven for another 10 minutes or until the leeks have softened. Remove from the oven and season to taste. Tuck the oysters under the leek mixture in the pan and return to the oven for another 10 minutes or until the edges of the oysters begin to curl. Serve in shallow pasta bowls or soup plates.

Serves 4

roasted baby octopus in sherry marinade

see variations page 222

Serve with a glass of chilled fino sherry to echo the marinade. Octopus needs high heat to cook quickly so it doesn't get rubbery, so it's best roasted or grilled.

for the sherry marinade
50 ml (2 fl oz) olive oil
50 ml (2 fl oz) dry sherry
6 garlic cloves, minced
1 tsp paprika
½ tsp fine sea salt

900 g (2 lb) baby octopus, cleaned
8 fresh plum tomatoes, cut in half
225 g (8 oz) pitted Kalamata or niçoise olives, cut in half
100 g (4 oz) pimento-stuffed green olives, drained and diced
25 g (1 oz) finely chopped fresh Italian parsley, to garnish

For the marinade, combine all the ingredients in a sealable plastic bag. Pour half the marinade into another container to reserve. Add the octopus to the marinade in the bag, seal and marinate in the refrigerator for up to 12 hours.

Preheat the oven to 230°C (450°F/Gas mark 8). Arrange the tomatoes in a roasting pan and drizzle with one quarter of the reserved marinade. Roast the tomatoes for 10 minutes or until beginning to soften and brown. Remove the octopus from the marinade, do not pat dry and place them with the tomatoes in the roasting pan. Return pan to the oven and roast for 3-5 minutes or until the octopus is white and opaque. Combine the octopus and tomatoes with the remaining reserved marinade and the olives. Portion onto plates and garnish with parsley.

Serves 8 as an appetiser

pecan-crusted catfish with roasted corn relish

see variations page 223

For a true taste of the Mississippi Delta, serve this colourful dish with cornbread.

for the roasted corn relish
450 g (1 lb) fresh corn kernels
225 g (8 oz) cherry tomatoes, halved
225 g (8 oz) chopped green or red pepper
100 g (4 oz) chopped green onion
50 ml (2 fl oz) olive oil, plus more
    for drizzling
2 tbsp red wine vinegar
fine sea salt and ground black pepper, to taste

225 g (8 oz) panko breadcrumbs
50 g (2 oz) chopped pecans
1 tbsp olive oil
2 tbsp water
fine sea salt and ground black pepper, to taste
4 skinless catfish fillets

Preheat the oven to 220°C (425°F/Gas mark 7). Place the corn, tomatoes, pepper and onion in a large bowl, and toss with olive oil and vinegar to coat. Season to taste. Arrange the corn relish in one layer on a rimmed baking tray. In a small bowl, mix the breadcrumbs, pecans, 1 tablespoon olive oil and water. Season to taste. Press the breadcrumb mixture onto the top of each catfish fillet. Arrange the catfish on the bed of corn relish, drizzle all with a little more olive oil and roast for 10–12 minutes or until the catfish begins to flake when tested with a fork in the thickest part.

Serves 4

roasted monkfish romesco

see variations page 224

Serve this dish with crusty bread to mop up all the delicious juices. Colourful Romesco, a classic sauce from Catalonia, also functions as a vegetable in this dish.

for the romesco
100 g (4 oz) almonds, toasted
1 slice white bread, toasted and crumbled
2 red peppers, roasted, deseeded and peeled
1 tbsp chopped fresh Italian parsley
2 cloves garlic, minced
1/2 tsp red pepper flakes
1/4 tsp sea salt
1/4 tsp freshly ground black pepper
75 ml (3 fl oz) red wine vinegar
150 ml (5 fl oz) extra-virgin olive oil

1 medium courgette, thinly sliced into rounds
1 red onion, thinly sliced into rounds
olive oil, for drizzling
fine sea salt and freshly ground black pepper, to taste
4 skinless monkfish fillets

To make the sauce, finely grind the almonds in a food processor. Add the toasted bread, peppers, parsley, garlic, pepper flakes, salt and pepper. Purée to form a smooth paste. Add the vinegar and blend. While the motor is running, slowly add the olive oil in a thin stream until all the ingredients are incorporated.

Preheat the oven to 220°C (425°F/Gas mark 7). Arrange the courgette and onion slices on a baking tray, drizzle with olive oil and season to taste. Place the fish fillets on the vegetables, drizzle with olive oil and season to taste. Roast for 10–12 minutes or until the monkfish begins to flake when tested with a fork in the thickest part. Serve with Romesco.

Serves 4

jamaican roast turbot

see variations page 225

With distinctive jerk seasoning, these whole roast fish take on the flavour of the islands. Scotch bonnet peppers are the hottest, so feel free to substitute jalapeño or serrano peppers if your tastebuds can't take the heat. Dat good eat!

for the jerk seasoning
1 medium yellow onion, chopped
4 green onions, chopped
4 sprigs fresh thyme or 2 tsp dried thyme
10 whole allspice berries
1 tbsp fine sea salt
1 tbsp ground black pepper

4 cloves garlic, minced
2 fresh scotch bonnet peppers, stemmed,
    deseeded and chopped
50 ml (2 fl oz) bottled pick-a-pepper sauce
4 small (450-g/1-lb) whole turbot, cleaned,
    with head and tail intact

Preheat the oven to 220°C (425°F/Gas mark 7). In a bowl, mix the jerk seasoning ingredients together. Stuff each fish with the seasoning mixture, place the fish on a baking tray and cover with foil. Roast for 30–35 minutes or until the fish begins to flake when tested with a fork in the thickest part.

Serves 4

pesce al forno

see variations page 226

Whole fish that are too small to grill, but too big to fry, work well with this traditional Italian oven method. They bake to a luscious, aromatic, crusty finish, so be sure to have lots of Italian bread to mop it all up.

700 g (1½ lb) whole, small fish, such as
    sardines, perch, smallmouth bass or
    mackerel, with head and tail intact
5 tbsp olive oil
2 bay leaves

4 tbsp panko or other dried breadcrumbs
25 g (1 oz) finely chopped fresh Italian parsley
1 tsp dried oregano
1 tsp grated lemon zest
100 ml (4 fl oz) dry white wine

Preheat the oven to 220°C (425°F/Gas mark 7). Cut the heads off the fish. Place each fish, cut-side down, on a flat surface and press down on fish with both hands to open like a book and flatten. With your fingers, remove the backbone, then cut off the tail. Drizzle 2 tablespoons of the olive oil in a baking dish and arrange the bay leaves on the bottom. Arrange the fish in dish, skin-side down, so that they fit snugly. In a bowl, combine remaining 3 tablespoons olive oil, breadcrumbs, parsley, oregano and lemon zest. Sprinkle this mixture over the fish and pour in the wine. Roast for 18–20 minutes or until the fish begin to flake when tested with a fork in the thickest part.

Serves 8–10

tangy roast bluefish with coriander & bay

see variations page 227

Oily fish, such as bluefish and mackerel, benefit from a touch of vinegar and aromatic herbs, as in this recipe, which starts out in a cold oven.

75 g (3 oz) unsalted butter, softened
20 bay leaves, snipped with scissors
2 tbsp whole coriander seeds
2 tbsp coarse sea salt
1 (1–1½ kg/3–4-lb) whole bluefish,
   cleaned, with head and tail intact

1 lemon, thinly sliced
225 g (8 fl oz) tarragon vinegar
6 whole black peppercorns
fine sea salt, to taste

Spread 2 tablespoons of the butter over the bottom of a roasting pan. In a bowl, combine the remaining butter, bay leaves, coriander seeds and salt. Spread the interior of the fish with half of the flavoured butter, then stuff with lemon slices. Place the fish diagonally in the roasting pan, turning the tail up and over if necessary to fit. Dot the fish with the remaining flavoured butter. Place in a cold oven and turn the temperature to 230°C (450°F/Gas mark 8). Roast for 40–45 minutes or until the fish begins to flake when tested with a fork in the thickest part.

Transfer the fish to a serving platter and tent with foil. Pour the juices from the roasting pan into a large saucepan over high heat. Stir in the vinegar, peppercorns and sea salt, and bring to the boil for 1 minute. Pour the hot sauce over the fish and serve.

Serves 4–6

basque-style roast fish

see variations page 228

From the Pyrenees to the Cantabrian Mountains, the Basque people prefer the wild mountains. Their unique cuisine makes the most of the lamb they raise as well as the fish they catch.

50 ml (2 fl oz) olive oil
2 medium onions, chopped
2 cloves garlic, minced
1 (100-g/4-oz) tin sliced pimentos
225 g (8 oz) chopped fresh or tinned
     tomatoes, drained

1 tsp smoked or Hungarian paprika
50 g (2 oz) chopped fresh Italian parsley
4 whole, small rainbow trout, cleaned, heads
     and tails removed
100 ml (4 fl oz) dry white wine

Preheat the oven to 220°C (425°F/Gas mark 7). In a bowl, mix the olive oil, onions, garlic, pimentos, tomatoes, paprika and parsley together. Stuff each fish with the mixture, place the fish in a large, oiled baking dish, pour in the wine and cover with foil. Roast for 30–35 minutes or until the fish begins to flake when tested with a fork in the thickest part.

Serves 4

korean roasted branzino

see variations page 229

Branzino, or European sea bass, is delicious when roasted. Prepared kimchee is a spicy Korean cabbage relish that is available in better supermarkets.

4 (175–225-g/6–8-oz) branzino fillets,
    rinsed and patted dry
450 g (1 lb) prepared kimchee,
    coarsely chopped

for the korean kochukaru sauce
50 ml (2 fl oz) soya sauce
1 tbsp sugar

1 tbsp rice wine
2 tsp sesame oil
2 tbsp kochukaru (Korean chilli pepper flakes)
fine sea salt and freshly ground black pepper,
    to taste

Preheat the oven to 220°C (425°F/Gas mark 7). Arrange the fillets on an oiled baking tray and top with the kimchee. Roast for 20–25 minutes or until the fish begins to flake when tested with a fork in the thickest part. In a saucepan, bring the soya sauce, sugar and rice wine to the boil. Stir to dissolve the sugar. Remove from the heat and stir in the sesame oil and chilli pepper flakes. Season to taste. Pour sauce over the fish and serve.

Serves 4

variations

simple roasted prawns & asparagus

see base recipe page 205

creole roasted prawns & pepper po' boy
Prepare basic recipe, seasoning prawns with Creole-style seasoning. Roast a
red, yellow and green pepper, deseeded and cut into strips, in place of asparagus.
Spread 4 rolls with Rémoulade (page 261). Divide roasted prawns and peppers
among the rolls, and top with shredded lettuce and sliced tomato to make
a sandwich.

simple roasted prawns & asparagus with orange hollandaise
Prepare basic recipe. Serve with Orange Hollandaise (page 276).

simple roasted scallops & asparagus
Prepare basic recipe, using medium scallops in place of prawns. Roast for
5–6 minutes or until they are almost opaque and firm to the touch.

roasted chipotle prawn bruschetta
Prepare basic recipe, omitting asparagus. Mix 50 g (2 oz) tinned squash purée,
50 g (2 oz) fresh goat cheese, 1 finely chopped, tinned chipotle pepper in
adobo sauce, 1 tablespoon honey and 1 tablespoon cider vinegar until well
blended. Spread on toasted bread, top with roasted prawns and garnish with
chopped coriander.

oyster pan roast with buttery leeks

see base recipe page 206

buttery oyster leek penne
Prepare the basic recipe, using very small oysters. Bring a large pan of salted water to the boil and cook 450 g (1 lb) penne until al dente. Drain and toss with the oyster pan roast and garnish with freshly grated Parmesan.

oyster pan roast with buttery leeks & new potatoes
Prepare the basic recipe, adding 225 g (8 oz) new potatoes, scrubbed and quartered, to the leek mixture before roasting.

oyster & leek chowder
Prepare the basic recipe. Stir 475 ml (16 fl oz) prepared Alfredo sauce into the roasted leek mixture, tuck the oysters under the leeks then return to the oven until the edges of the oysters have curled and the soup is hot. Ladle into bowls and serve with savoury biscuits.

pan-roasted prawns with buttery leeks
Prepare the basic recipe, using 100 ml (4 fl oz) dry white wine in place of oyster juices and 450 g (1 lb) peeled and deveined large prawns in place of oysters.

variations

roasted baby octopus in sherry marinade

see base recipe page 209

roasted baby cuttlefish in sherry marinade
Prepare the basic recipe, using baby cuttlefish in place of octopus.

roasted baby squid in sherry marinade
Prepare the basic recipe, using baby squid, heads removed, in place of octopus.

roasted prawns in sherry marinade
Prepare the basic recipe, using peeled and deveined large prawns in place of
octopus. Roast for 5–7 minutes or until the prawns turn pink and opaque.

roasted scallops in sherry marinade
Prepare the basic recipe, using medium scallops in place of octopus. Add
225 g (8 oz) chopped courgette and 1 coarsely chopped red onion, drizzled with
olive oil and seasoned to taste, to the tomatoes before roasting them.

pecan-crusted catfish with roasted corn relish

see base recipe page 210

roasted pecan-crusted tilapia with basil aïoli
Prepare the basic recipe, omitting the corn relish, and serve topped with
Basil Aïoli (page 197).

roasted almond-crusted salmon with roasted corn relish
Prepare the basic recipe, using salmon in place of catfish and chopped almonds in
place of pecans.

roasted halibut with roasted red pepper relish
Prepare the basic recipe, using halibut in place of catfish and chopped red pepper in
place of corn.

roasted hake with artichoke glaze
Prepare the basic recipe, using hake fillets in place of catfish and Artichoke Glaze
(page 184) in place of the breadcrumb-pecan topping.

variations

roasted monkfish with romesco

see base recipe page 212

roasted prawns with romesco
Prepare the basic recipe, using peeled and deveined large prawns in place of monkfish. Roast for 8–10 minutes or until the prawns are pink and opaque.

roasted halibut with romesco
Prepare the basic recipe, using halibut in place of monkfish.

roasted monkfish soup with rouille
Prepare the basic recipe, using Rouille (page 275) in place of Romesco. Serve the roasted vegetables and fish in shallow bowls, topped with hot prepared fish stock. Dollop with the Rouille.

roasted monkfish & prawns soup with rouille
Prepare the basic recipe, using half monkfish and half peeled and deveined large prawns and Rouille (page 275) in place of Romesco. Roast for 8–10 minutes or until the prawns are pink and opaque. Serve the roasted vegetables and seafood in shallow bowls, topped with hot fish stock. Dollop with the Rouille.

variations

jamaican roast turbot

see base recipe page 213

spanish roast turbot in sherry marinade
Prepare basic recipe, omitting jerk seasoning. Make a stuffing with
Sherry Marinade (page 209), 225 g (8 oz) chopped pitted Kalamata olives
and 225 g (8 oz) chopped pimento-stuffed green olives. Stuff each fish,
cover and roast.

french roast turbot
Prepare basic recipe, omitting jerk seasoning. Stuff each fish with 4 sprigs
tarragon, 4 lemon slices, salt and pepper, then drizzle inside and out with
25 g (1 oz) melted butter. Cover and roast.

roast turbot with parsley sauce
Prepare the basic recipe, omitting jerk seasoning. Stuff each fish with
4 sprigs Italian parsley, 4 lemon slices, salt and pepper, then drizzle inside
and out with 25 g (1 oz) melted butter. Cover and roast. Warm 475 ml
(16 fl oz) prepared Alfredo sauce and stir in 25 g (1 oz) chopped fresh
Italian parsley. Serve with roast fish.

roasted jerk salmon
Prepare basic recipe, using a whole salmon fillet spread with jerk seasoning.
Cover and roast for 20 minutes or until the fish begins to flake when tested
with a fork in the thickest part.

variations

pesce al forno

see base recipe page 214

italian roast fish fillets
Prepare the basic recipe, using 700 g (1½ lb) fish fillets in place of small whole fish. Roast for 10–12 minutes or until the fish begins to flake when tested with a fork in the thickest part.

italian roast prawns
Prepare the basic recipe, using 700 g (1½ lb) whole, large prawns, peeled and deveined, in place of fish. Roast for 8–10 minutes or until the prawns are pink and opaque.

venetian roast lobster
Prepare the basic recipe, using 4 rock lobster tails. Have your fishmonger dispatch live lobster and cut the lobster tails for you; do not butterfly. Arrange them in the dish with the other ingredients. Roast for 10–12 minutes, or until the lobster meat is white and opaque and the shells are red.

italian roast large fish
Prepare the basic recipe, using 1 large whole fish in place of the small fish. Roast for 20–22 minutes or until the fish begins to flake when tested with a fork in the thickest part.

tangy roast bluefish with coriander & bay

see base recipe page 216

tangy roast mackerel with coriander & bay
Prepare the basic recipe, using mackerel in place of bluefish.

tangy roast sardines with coriander & bay
Prepare the basic recipe, using large sardines in place of bluefish. Roast for 30–35 minutes or until the sardines flake when tested with a fork in the thickest part.

roast amberjack in sherry marinade
Instead of the basic recipe, use Sherry Marinade (page 209) and amberjack in place of bluefish. Brush the fish, inside and out with the marinade, then pour the rest of it around the fish. Roast for 30–35 minutes or until the fish begins to flake when tested with a fork in the thickest part.

tangy roast kingfish with coriander & bay
Prepare the basic recipe, using kingfish in place of bluefish.

variations

basque-style roast fish

see base recipe page 217

bacon-wrapped roast trout
Prepare the basic recipe, wrapping each trout with a slice of bacon before cooking. Remove the foil during the last 10 minutes of cooking to crisp the bacon.

tapas-style roast fish
Prepare the basic recipe, using Tapas Topping (page 186) to stuff the fish in place of the olive oil, onions, garlic, tomatoes, pimentos and parsley.

asian roast trout
Prepare the basic recipe, using a mixture of 100 g (4 oz) chopped green onion, 100 g (4 oz) fermented black beans and 2 tablespoons grated fresh root ginger to stuff the fish in place of the olive oil, onions, garlic, tomatoes, pimentos and parsley. Use sake or rice wine in place of dry white wine.

easy mexican roast trout
Prepare the basic recipe, using 475 ml (16 fl oz) freshly prepared tomato salsa to stuff the fish in place of the olive oil, onions, garlic, tomatoes, pimentos and parsley. Use tequila in place of dry white wine.

korean roasted branzino

see base recipe page 218

korean branzino en papillote
Prepare the basic recipe, but instead of the baking pan, place each fillet on a 40-cm (16-in) square of parchment paper before topping with kimchee and wrap like a parcel. Roast for 20 minutes. Pass the sauce at the table.

oven-roasted whitefish with three-pepper butter
Prepare the basic recipe, using whitefish in place of branzino and omitting sauce. Instead of the baking pan, place each fillet on a 40-cm (16-in) square of parchment paper. Add 50 g (2 oz) each chopped red, green and yellow pepper to prepared Onion Butter (page 192). Spread on the fish and wrap like a parcel before roasting.

roasted orange roughy with lemon-tarragon butter
Prepare the basic recipe, using orange roughy in place of branzino and Lemon-Tarragon Butter (page 190) in place of kimchee. Omit the sauce.

roasted branzino with tapas topping
Prepare the basic recipe, using Tapas Topping (page 186) in place of kimchee. Omit the sauce.

in the smoker

For centuries, fish and shellfish were salted and dried or smoked to preserve them during the cold months when fishing was too perilous. Today, we love smoked seafood because it tastes so wonderful and in so many ways – from centre-of-the-plate fillets to the smoky heart of soups, stews and savory dips.

leaf-wrapped smoked prawns with rémoulade

see variations page 246

The classic prawn cocktail just got a lot more interesting!

24 large prawns, peeled and deveined, rinsed and patted dry
24 fresh baby spinach leaves, rinsed and patted dry
olive oil, for brushing
fine sea salt, to taste

6 (30-cm/12-in) bamboo skewers, soaked in water for 30 minutes
handful dry wood chips, such as mesquite, hickory or alder
Rémoulade (page 261), to serve

Prepare an indirect fire in your barbecue (with a fire on one side and no fire on the other). Wrap each prawn around the middle in a spinach leaf and thread onto the soaked wooden skewers. Brush with olive oil and season with salt. For a charcoal barbecue, throw the dry wood chips on the coals. For a gas barbecue, make a packet out of aluminium foil to contain the chips, poke holes in the packet and place by a gas burner. Place the skewers on the indirect (no heat) side of the barbecue. When you see the first wisp of smoke, close the lid. Smoke for 20–30 minutes or until the prawns have a burnished pink appearance and are opaque. Serve with the Rémoulade.

Serves 6

smoked oyster po' boy sandwich

see variations page 247

Oysters take on a more complex flavour when they're hot-smoked. Use larger varieties like Blue Point or Kumamoto for this recipe.

12 shucked oysters, rinsed and patted dry
olive oil, for brushing
fine sea salt
handful dry wood chips, such as mesquite,
    hickory or alder

4 rolls or hot dog buns
Rémoulade (261)
450 g (1 lb) shredded lettuce
2 fresh tomatoes, thinly sliced

Prepare an indirect fire in your barbecue (a fire on one side and no fire on the other). Brush the oysters with olive oil, season with salt and place in a disposable aluminium pan. For a charcoal barbecue, throw the dry wood chips on the coals. For a gas barbecue, make a packet out of aluminium foil to hold the chips, poke holes in the packet and place by a gas burner. Place the oyster pan on the indirect (no heat) side of the barbecue. When you see the first wisp of smoke, close the lid. Smoke for 20–30 minutes or until the oysters have a burnished appearance and the edges have curled. Split and toast the rolls on the hot side of the barbecue. Spread the inside of the rolls with Rémoulade. Top the bottom roll with shredded lettuce and thinly sliced tomatoes. Arrange the hot oysters on top of the tomatoes, replace the top bun and serve.

Serves 4

smoked scallops with tomato-spinach orzo

see variations page 248

The slight bitterness from wood smoke makes a fine counterpoint to the natural sweetness of scallops. Serve them on a bed of colourful pasta that is both sauce and side dish.

12 large callops, rinsed and patted dry
olive oil, for brushing
fine sea salt, to taste

handful dry wood chips, such as mesquite, hickory or alder
Tomato-Spinach Orzo (page 268), to serve

Prepare an indirect fire in your barbecue (a fire on one side and no fire on the other). Brush the oysters with olive oil, season with salt and place in a disposable aluminium pan. For a charcoal barbecue, throw the dry wood chips on the coals. For a gas barbecue, make a packet out of aluminium foil to contain the chips, poke holes in the packet and place by a gas burner. Place the oysters on the indirect (no heat) side of the barbecue. When you see the first wisp of smoke, close the lid. Smoke for 20–30 minutes or until the scallops have a burnished appearance and are opaque. Serve the scallops atop Tomato-Spinach Orzo.

Serves 4

smoked mussels with frites & aïoli

see variations page 249

In this new take on the classic Belgian dish of steamed mussels paired with crisp French fries and homemade mayonnaise, you both smoke and barbecue the mussels over high heat, so they open. Make sure you scrub away the 'beard' from each mussel. Discard any that are open before you smoke them as well as any that don't open after smoking.

1½ kg (3 lb) mussels, scrubbed, with
   beards removed
handful dry wood chips, such as mesquite,
   hickory or alder

25 g (1 oz) chopped fresh Italian parsley,
   to garnish
Frites (page 269), to serve
Aïoli (page 262), to serve

Prepare an indirect fire in your barbecue (a fire on one side and no fire on the other). Place the mussels in a disposable aluminium pan. For a charcoal barbecue, throw the dry wood chips on the coals. For a gas barbecue, make a packet out of aluminium foil to hold the chips, poke holes in the packet and place by a gas burner. Place the oysters on the direct (high heat) side of the barbecue. When you see the first wisp of smoke, close the lid. Smoke for 10–15 minutes or until the mussels have opened and have a smoky aroma. Serve the mussels, garnished with parsley, in bowls accompanied by Frites and Aïoli.

Serves 4

apple-smoked salmon

see variations page 250

A barbecue-smoked salmon fillet, served on a platter, can be the eye-catching centrepiece of a brunch, lunch or casual get-together. This looks wonderful on a platter, garnished with thinly sliced lemons and fresh dill sprigs.

1 (700–900-g/1½–2 lb) boneless, skinless
   salmon fillet
1 (325-g/12-oz) bottle zesty Italian dressing

100 g (4 oz) Cajun-style seafood seasoning or
   dry rub of your choice
handful dry wood chips, such as apple

Place the salmon fillet in a plastic container or zipper-top plastic bag. Pour the Italian dressing into the bag. Cover and marinate the fillet for 3–4 hours in the refrigerator. Remove the salmon from the marinade (do not pat dry) and discard the marinade. Sprinkle the seasoning or dry rub on the top of the fish.

Prepare an indirect fire in your barbecue (a fire on one side and no fire on the other). For a charcoal barbecue, throw the dry wood chips on the coals. For a gas barbecue, make a packet out of aluminium foil to hold the chips, poke holes in the packet and place by a gas burner. Place the salmon on the indirect (no heat) side of the barbecue. When you see the first wisp of smoke, close the lid. Smoke for 45–60 minutes or until the salmon is burnished, has a smoky aroma and begins to flake when tested with a fork in the thickest part. Serve on a platter, garnished as desired and use leftover salmon in any of the recipe variations on page 250.

Serves 8

smoked trout with fresh herb butter

see variations page 251

Hot smoked trout is fabulous. It has a smoky aroma, a delicate and moist texture and fabulous flavour. It looks wonderful when garnished with thinly sliced lemons and sprigs of fresh herbs. Use any leftovers in pâté, for breakfast with eggs or in sandwiches.

4 (450-g/1-lb) whole trout, dressed, rinsed
    and patted dry
Fresh Herb Butter (page 272)

handful dry wood chips, such as hickory, oak
    or pecan

Open each trout like a book and spread with some of the herb butter, inside and out. Prepare an indirect fire in your barbecue (a fire on one side and no fire on the other). For a charcoal barbecue, throw the dry wood chips on the coals. For a gas barbecue, make a packet out of aluminium foil to contain the chips, poke holes in the packet and place by a gas burner. Place the trout on the indirect (no heat) side of the barbecue. When you see the first wisp of smoke, close the lid. Smoke for 45–60 minutes or until the trout are burnished, have a smoky aroma and begin to flake when tested with a fork in the thickest part. Serve on a platter, garnished as desired and use leftovers in variations on page 251.

Serves 4

maple-smoked whitefish with butternut squash, sage & parmesan orzo

see variations page 252

Fisheries around the Great Lakes sell lots of fresh whitefish, lake perch and chubs in good weather. They also smoke their catch for winter use, using local maple hardwood. You can do the same on your barbecue. Serve the succulent whitefish with another cold weather dish, Butternut Squash, Sage & Parmesan Orzo.

4 (225-g/8-oz) whitefish fillets, rinsed and
    patted dry
canola oil, for brushing
fine sea salt and ground black pepper, to taste

handful dry wood chips, such as hickory,
    oak or pecan
Butternut Squash, Sage & Parmesan Orzo
    (page 279), to serve

Brush the fish with oil and season to taste. Oil a perforated barbecue rack or disposable aluminium baking tray and place the fish on it. Prepare an indirect fire in your barbecue (a fire on one side and no fire on the other). For a charcoal barbecue, throw the dry wood chips on the coals. For a gas barbecue, make a packet out of aluminium foil to hold the chips, poke holes in the packet and place by a gas burner. Place the fish on the indirect (no heat) side of the barbecue. At the first wisp of smoke, close the lid. Smoke for 15–20 minutes or until the fish is burnished, has a smoky aroma and begins to flake when tested with a fork in the thickest part. Serve with the Orzo.

Serves 8–10

smoked haddock with hollandaise

see variations page 253

Known as 'finnan haddie' in Scotland, smoked haddock is usually cold-smoked. This hot-smoked version, paired with luscious Hollandaise (page 264), mimics a classic French dish served at brasseries along the Atlantic coast.

4 haddock fillets, rinsed and patted dry
olive oil, for brushing
fine sea salt and freshly ground black pepper,
    to taste

handful dry wood chips, such as hickory,
    oak or pecan
Blender Hollandaise (page 264)

Brush the fish with oil and season to taste. Oil a perforated barbecue rack or disposable aluminium baking tray and place the fish on it. Prepare an indirect fire in your barbecue (a fire on one side and no fire on the other). For a charcoal barbecue, throw the dry wood chips on the coals. For a gas barbecue, make a packet out of aluminium foil to contain the chips, poke holes in the packet and place by a gas burner. Place the fish on the indirect (no heat) side of the barbecue. When you see the first wisp of smoke, close the lid. Smoke for 20–30 minutes or until the fish is burnished, has a smoky aroma and begins to flake when tested with a fork in the thickest part. To serve, spoon the Hollandaise over each fillet.

Serves 4

cape kedgeree

see variations page 254

Kedgeree, dating from British colonial days, is a brunch dish made with flaked, smoked fish, cooked rice, hard-boiled eggs, fresh herbs and a white sauce to bind it all together. Some people like to add a dash of curry powder. When made with hot-smoked fish, this dish is divine. Although smoked haddock is the usual fish for kedgeree, you can also use salmon, trout or whitefish.

75 g (3 oz) butter
1 tbsp chopped onion
3 tbsp plain flour
475 ml (16 fl oz) milk
1 tsp curry powder (optional)
450 g (1 lb) flaked, smoked haddock (page 242)

2 large eggs, hard-boiled and finely chopped
450 g (1 lb) cooked white rice
50 g (2 oz) chopped fresh Italian parsley
fine sea salt and freshly ground black pepper,
    to taste

Melt the butter in a large saucepan over medium-high heat, then sauté the onion until transparent, about 4 minutes. Stir in the flour and cook, stirring, for 2 minutes. Whisk in the milk and cook, whisking constantly, until the sauce thickens, about 5 minutes. Stir in the optional curry powder, haddock, eggs, rice and parsley until well combined. Season to taste and serve hot.

Serves 4

bayou smoked catfish 'n' corn

see variations page 255

This Mississippi Delta recipe is easy to do. Fire up your barbecue. Slice the kernels off ears of fresh uncooked corn so they stay together in 'planks'. Brush the corn and fish with oil and season with Cajun spices. Then smoke to a burnished goodness.

4 catfish fillets, rinsed and patted dry	50 ml (2 fl oz) olive oil
4 ears fresh corn, the kernels sliced off with a sharp knife in 'planks'	1 tbsp Cajun seasoning or to taste

Brush the fish and corn with oil and season to taste. Oil a perforated barbecue rack or disposable aluminium baking tray and place the fish and corn on it. Prepare an indirect fire in your barbecue (a fire on one side and no fire on the other). For a charcoal barbecue, throw the dry wood chips on the coals. For a gas barbecue, make a packet out of aluminium foil to hold the chips, poke holes in the packet and place by a gas burner. Place the fish on the indirect (no heat) side of the barbecue. When you see the first wisp of smoke, close the lid. Smoke for 20–30 minutes or until the fish is burnished, has a smoky aroma and begins to flake when tested with a fork in the thickest part.

Serves 4

variations

leaf-wrapped smoked prawns with rémoulade

see base recipe page 231

leaf-wrapped hob-smoked prawns with rémoulade

Prepare basic recipe, using a hob smoker. Place 1 rounded tablespoonful of fine, dry wood chips in the centre of the bottom of smoker. Cover with the deflector pan, then the rack. Place skewers on rack and slide cover almost closed. Place smoker over medium-high heat. At the first wisp of smoke, close the lid all the way. Smoke for 8 minutes or until prawns are burnished pink and opaque.

leaf-wrapped smoked prawns with tarragon hollandaise

Prepare basic recipe, using Tarragon Hollandaise (page 276) in place of Rémoulade.

leaf-wrapped smoked prawns with cocktail sauce

Prepare basic recipe, using Classic Cocktail Sauce (page 49) in place of Rémoulade.

open-face smoked prawns sandwiches with tarragon hollandaise

Prepare basic recipe, omitting Rémoulade. Brush 4 slices of crusty bread, then barbecue on both sides to get good barbecue marks. Top with smoked prawns. Combine 100 g (4 oz) chopped fresh tomato, 100 g (4 oz) chopped pitted Kalamata olives and 2 tablespoons capers. Top prawns with Tarragon Hollandaise (page 276) then some tomato mixture.

variations

smoked oyster po' boy sandwich

see base recipe page 232

smoked prawns po' boy sandwich
Prepare basic recipe, using 24 smoked prawns in place of oysters.

smoked scallop po' boy sandwich
Prepare basic recipe, using 12 smoked scallops in place of oysters.

hob-smoked oysters
Prepare basic recipe, using a hob smoker in place of a barbecue. Place 1 rounded tablespoonful of fine, dry wood chips in the centre of the bottom of the stovetop smoker. Cover with the deflector pan, then the rack. Place oysters on the rack and slide the cover almost closed. Place smoker over medium-high heat. At the first wisp of smoke, close the lid all the way. Smoke for 8 minutes or until oysters are burnished and opaque.

smoked oyster stew
Prepare basic recipe. Add smoked oysters to Oyster Stew (page 84), replacing 1 dozen fresh oysters, during the last 5 minutes of cooking.

smoked scallops with tomato–spinach orzo

see base recipe page 235

smoked scallops with mango salsa

Prepare basic recipe, using Mango & Lime Salsa (page 265) in place of Orzo.

hob-smoked scallops with tomato–spinach orzo

Prepare basic recipe, using a hob smoker in place of a barbecue. Place 1 rounded tablespoonful of fine, dry wood chips in the centre of the smoker's bottom. Cover with the deflector pan, then the rack. Place the oysters on the rack and slide the cover almost closed. Place the smoker over medium-high heat. When you see the first wisp of smoke, close the lid all the way. Smoke for 8 minutes or until the scallops are burnished and opaque.

smoked scallop pasta with bistro butter

Prepare basic recipe, using 450 g (1 lb) bay scallops in place of sea scallops. Smoke for 15 minutes. Toss the smoked scallops with 450 g (1 lb) cooked penne and Bistro Butter (page 272) in place of Orzo.

smoked scallop chowder

Prepare basic recipe, using 450 g (1 lb) bay scallops in place of sea scallops. Smoke for 15 minutes. Add scallops in place of clams in Clam Chowder (page 76).

smoked mussels with frites & aïoli

see base recipe page 236

smoked mussels vinaigrette
Prepare the basic recipe recipe, omitting the Frites and Aïoli. Remove the mussels from the shells and toss with Herbed Tomato Vinaigrette (page 258). Serve over baby greens.

smoked mussels with barbecued bread & ancho butter
Prepare the basic recipe, omitting the Frites and Aïoli. Brush slices of crusty bread with Ancho-Lime Butter (page 257), barbecue on both sides for good barbecue marks and serve with mussels.

smoked mussel chowder
Prepare the basic recipe, omitting the Frites and Aïoli. Remove the mussels from the shells and add to Clam Chowder (page 76), in place of clams, during the last 5 minutes of cooking.

smoked mussel pasta with basil aïoli
Prepare the basic recipe, omitting the Frites. Remove the mussels from the shells. Toss the smoked mussels with 450 g (1 lb) cooked penne and Basil Aïoli (page 197).

variations

apple-smoked salmon

see base recipe page 238

apple-smoked salmon pâté
Prepare basic recipe. In a food processor, process 100 g (4 oz) flaked smoked salmon, 100 g (4 oz) softened unsalted butter, 1 tablespoon chopped fresh dill and 1 teaspoon grated lemon zest until smooth. Serve the pâté in a crock, garnished with more chopped fresh dill and surrounded with sesame crackers or slices of French or pumpernickel bread.

smoked salmon cakes
Prepare basic recipe. Use leftover salmon in place of crabmeat in basic Crab Cakes (page 105).

smoked salmon aïoli salad
Prepare basic recipe. Place the smoked salmon atop 900 g (2 lb) greens on a platter. Serve a bowl of Aïoli on the side. (page 262).

smoked salmon scrambled eggs
Prepare basic recipe. Whisk 6 large eggs with 2 tablespoons cream, 2 tablespoons snipped fresh chives and salt and pepper, to taste. Melt 25 g (1 oz) butter in a large, nonstick frying pan. Add egg mixture and 100 g (4 oz) flaked, smoked salmon fillet. Cook until softly scrambled. Garnish with more snipped chives and soured cream.

variations

smoked trout with fresh herb butter

see base recipe page 239

smoked trout scrambled eggs
Prepare basic recipe. Whisk 6 large eggs with 2 tablespoons cream,
2 tablespoons snipped fresh chives, salt and pepper. Melt 25 g (1 oz) butter in
a large frying pan. Add egg mixture and 100 g (4 oz) flaked, smoked trout and
softly scramble. Garnish with snipped chives and soured cream.

smoked trout salad
Prepare basic recipe. Serve smoked trout fillets over baby greens and steamed
new potatoes. Drizzle with Lemon-Dill Vinaigrette (page 273) before serving.

smoked trout pâté
Prepare basic recipe. Place 100 g (4 oz) flaked smoked trout in a food
processor. Add 100 g (4 oz) softened unsalted butter, 1 tablespoon chopped
fresh dill and 1 teaspoon grated lemon zest. Process until smooth. Serve pâté,
garnished with fresh dill, in a crock with sesame crackers or slices of French or
pumpernickel bread.

smoked trout with horseradish cream
Prepare basic recipe. Chill leftover fillets and serve on baby greens. Dollop with
mixture of 100 ml (4 fl oz) soured cream, 100 ml (4 fl oz) heavy cream and
prepared horseradish to taste.

variations

maple-smoked whitefish with butternut squash, sage & parmesan orzo

see base recipe page 240

maple-smoked whitefish beignets
Prepare the basic recipe, omitting the Orzo. Use the maple-smoked whitefish in place of fresh whitefish in the basic Whitefish Beignets recipe (page 102).

maple-smoked whitefish & wild rice salad
Prepare the basic recipe, omitting the Orzo. Flake 230 g (8 oz) of the fish and combine it with 145 g (5 oz) cooked wild rice, 220 g (8 oz) mayonnaise, 80 g (3 oz) chopped green onion, 60 g (2 oz) toasted pecans, and salt and ground white pepper to taste.

maple-smoked whitefish soup
Prepare the basic recipe. Combine 230 g (8 oz) flaked, leftover whitefish with 170 g (6 oz) leftover Orzo and 470 ml (1 pt) chicken broth. Bring to a simmer and serve hot.

maple-smoked walleye pike with butternut squash, sage & parmesan orzo
Prepare the basic recipe, using walleye pike in place of whitefish.

variations

smoked haddock with hollandaise

see base recipe page 242

smoked haddock with orange hollandaise
Prepare the basic recipe, using Orange Hollandaise (page 276) in place of Blender Hollandaise.

smoked cod with hollandaise
Prepare the basic recipe, using cod in place of haddock.

prosciutto-wrapped haddock
Prepare the basic recipe, wrapping each fillet with a piece of prosciutto and securing with a toothpick before smoking.

smoked haddock with roasted red pepper & basil purée
Prepare the basic recipe, serving each fillet over Roasted Red Pepper & Basil Purée (page 164).

variations

cape kedgeree

see base recipe page 243

cape kedgeree with apple-smoked salmon
Prepare the basic recipe, using apple-smoked salmon (page 238) in place of the haddock.

cape kedgeree with maple-smoked whitefish
Prepare the basic recipe, using maple-smoked whitefish (page 240) in place of the haddock.

kedgeree cakes
Prepare the basic recipe. The next day, take any leftover kedgeree and form the mixture into cakes. Dip in beaten egg, then in plain flour and fry in butter until browned on both sides.

kedgeree-stuffed tomatoes
Prepare the basic recipe. Stem and remove half of the interiors of 8 ripe, large tomatoes. Fill with the kedgeree, garnish with parsley and serve hot or cold.

variations

bayou smoked catfish 'n' corn

see base recipe page 244

hot smoked catfish dip
Prepare basic recipe, omitting corn. Prepare Classic Crab Dip (page 127),
using 450 g (1 lb) smoked catfish in place of crab.

low-country smoked catfish & rice
Prepare basic recipe, omitting corn. Flake 450 g (1 lb) fish and use in place
of haddock in Cape Kedgeree (page 243). Use Cajun seasoning in place of
curry powder.

bayou smoked catfish 'n' corn salad
Prepare basic recipe. Flake 225 g (8 oz) catfish and combine with 225 g
(8 oz) smoked corn, 225 g (8 oz) mayonnaise, 100 g (4 oz) chopped green
onion, 100 g (4 oz) chopped red pepper and salt and ground white pepper,
to taste. Serve immediately or cover and chill.

bayou smoked catfish 'n' corn soup
Prepare basic recipe. Flake 225 g (8 oz) catfish. Stir into 1 L (1½ pt) boiling
chicken stock with 225 g (8 oz) smoked corn; 225 g (8 oz) chopped, cooked
andouille or chorizo sausage; and 225 g (8 oz) chopped tinned tomatoes.
Simmer for 15 minutes, then taste for seasoning. Serve garnished with
chopped green onions.

sauces & sides

Some things just naturally go with the delicate or
briny flavour of seafood. From the classic
hollandaise and flavoured butters to coleslaw
and salsas, seafood meals just taste better with
their accompaniments.

ancho-lime butter

see variations page 272

This delicious compound butter goes well with any grilled fish or shellfish. Place a pat or dollop of it on seafood when it's hot off the barbecue.

225 g (8 oz) unsalted butter, room temperature
1 tsp ground ancho
50 g (2 oz) chopped fresh coriander leaves

1 clove garlic, minced
2 tsp fresh lime juice

In a bowl, combine all the ingredients. Serve immediately or roll into a log and wrap in clingfilm. It will keep, refrigerated, for about a week. Frozen and wrapped in additional freezer clingfilm, the butter will keep for about 3 months.

Makes about 225 g (8 oz)

herbed tomato vinaigrette

see variations page 273

Use full-flavoured vinaigrettes like this one to drizzle over any cooked fish or shellfish. Finish the dish with a sprinkling of fresh herbs or baby greens.

450 g (1 lb) coarsely chopped fresh or tinned
    plum tomatoes, drained
100 g (4 oz) fresh Italian parsley
50 g (2 oz) fresh coriander
50 g (2 oz) fresh mint
2 tbsp fresh oregano
50 g (2 oz) chopped yellow onion

3 peeled garlic cloves
$^1/_2$ tsp cayenne pepper
1 tsp fine sea salt
1 tsp freshly ground black pepper
75 ml (3 fl oz) olive oil
75 ml (3 fl oz) sherry vinegar
25 ml (1 fl oz) water

Place all ingredients in a food processor and process until smooth. (The vinaigrette is best served the same day but will keep, covered, in the refrigerator for up to 5 days.)

Makes about 475 ml (1 pt)

rémoulade

see variations page 274

Rémoulade, a French sauce, is popular all over the world with seafood, French fries and sandwiches. Its tart, savoury yet smooth character pairs especially well with shellfish.

1 tsp finely chopped fresh Italian parsley
1 tsp grated onion
2 hard-boiled large egg yolks
1 tsp anchovy paste
1 clove garlic, minced

1 large organic egg or equivalent egg substitute
225 ml (8 fl oz) extra-virgin olive oil
2 tbsp capers, rinsed, drained and patted dry
juice of ½ lemon, or to your taste

To make the rémoulade, place the parsley, onion, hard-boiled egg yolks, anchovy paste, garlic and whole egg in a food processor or blender. Process into a paste. With the machine running, slowly add the olive oil in a thin stream through the feed tube until the mixture forms a mayonnaise-like consistency. Fold in the capers and lemon juice. Cover tightly and chill until ready to serve. (You may make the rémoulade up to 24 hours in advance.)

Makes about 325 ml (12 fl oz)

aïoli

see variations page 275

An aïoli is a garlicky mayonnaise, first beloved by Provençal cooks and now spread throughout the world. If you are concerned about the use of raw eggs in this sauce, make the Easy Aïoli variation or use egg substitute.

4 large fresh organic egg yolks
4–6 cloves garlic, minced
¼ tsp fine sea salt

¼ tsp freshly ground black pepper
325 ml (12 fl oz) extra-virgin olive oil

In a food processor, combine the egg yolks, garlic, salt and pepper. While the motor is running, slowly add the olive oil in a thin stream, creating a mayonnaise-like consistency. Keep refrigerated for 3–4 days.

Makes about 375 ml (14 fl oz)

blender hollandaise

see variations page 276

Serve this wonderful all-purpose sauce on hot grilled, baked, smoked, roasted – you name it – seafood. This recipe is made in the blender or food processor for a quick and easy version of the classic French sauce.

6 large fresh organic egg yolks
2 tbsp fresh lemon juice
1 tsp dry mustard
225 g (8 oz) unsalted butter, melted and
    still hot

$1/4$ tsp cayenne pepper, or to taste
fine sea salt, to taste

Place the egg yolks, lemon juice and mustard in a food processor or blender and process until smooth. Drizzle in the hot melted butter, pulsing the food processor or with the blender on low speed, until the sauce thickens. Add the cayenne and season with salt. Keep warm in the top of a double boiler or transfer to a stainless steel bowl and set over a pan of hot, not boiling, water until ready to serve.

Makes about 325 ml (12 fl oz)

mango & lime salsa

see variations page 277

Tropical mangoes and fresh lime combine to make a fresh salsa that is delicious with grilled fish and shellfish.

2 cloves garlic, minced
50 g (2 oz) finely chopped onion
1 fresh jalapeño pepper, stemmed, deseeded
   and finely chopped

25 g (1 oz) chopped fresh coriander
450 g (1 lb) chopped peeled mango
juice of 1 lime, or more to taste
salt and pepper, to taste

Combine all ingredients in a bowl. Season to taste and let sit at room temperature until ready to serve. The salsa will keep, covered, in the refrigerator for up to 3 days. Let it come to room temperature before serving.

Makes about 475 ml (16 fl oz)

baja slaw

see variations page 278

Fresh-tasting and colourful, this slaw goes well with steamed, fried or baked seafood.

450g (1 lb) shredded red cabbage
450 g (1 lb) shredded napa cabbage
6 green onions, finely chopped with some of
    the green
50 ml (2 fl oz) tarragon vinegar

50 ml (2 fl oz) soured cream
juice of 1 lime
juice of 1 lemon
salt and freshly ground black pepper, to taste

In a large bowl, combine the cabbages and green onions. In a small bowl, combine the vinegar, soured cream and lime and lemon juices. Season to taste. Pour the vinegar mixture over the cabbage and onion mixture and toss to blend. Serve immediately.

Serves 6–8

tomato-spinach orzo

see variations page 279

This colourful pasta dish, made with tiny orzo, can be served hot or cold.

450 g (1 lb) orzo, cooked according to package
  directions and drained
450 g (1 lb) baby spinach or larger-leafed
  spinach, torn into small pieces
500 ml (1 pt) cherry or grape tomatoes, sliced
  in half

100 g (4 oz) feta cheese, crumbled
4 tbsp olive oil
1 tbsp fresh lemon juice
2 cloves garlic, minced
fine sea salt and freshly ground black pepper,
  to taste

In a large bowl, combine the hot cooked orzo with the spinach, tomatoes and feta. In a small bowl, whisk the olive oil, lemon juice and garlic together. Season dressing to taste with the salt and pepper, then pour over the orzo and vegetables and toss to blend. Serve right away, at room temperature, or chilled.

Serves 4

frites

see variations page 280

Something hot and crispy – like frites or French fries – goes with fish and shellfish like, well, fish and chips! The secret to great frites is to cook them in two stages – once to eliminate moisture and the second time to get them crispy and golden brown.

2 L (3½ pt) canola oil
900 g (2 lb) medium baking potatoes, peeled
fine sea salt

Heat 5 cm (2 in) oil in a deep fryer or deep saucepan to 170°C (325°F). While the oil is heating, cut the potatoes into ½-cm (¼-in) sticks. Fry the potatoes in batches for 1½ minutes for each batch. They will be partially cooked, but not golden. Transfer with a slotted spoon to paper towels to drain.

When all the potatoes have been cooked once, increase the temperature to 180°C (350°F). Again, fry the potatoes in batches for about 5 minutes each time or until they are crispy and golden brown. Transfer with a slotted spoon to paper towels to drain and season to taste.

Serves 6

coconut rice

see variations page 281

With its taste of the tropics, this rice dish is wonderful with barbecued, steamed, fried, baked or roasted seafood. You can find the coconut and the curry leaves at Asian markets or health food stores.

475 ml (16 fl oz) water
1 tsp fine sea salt
225 g (8 oz) long-grain rice
$\frac{1}{2}$ tsp mustard seeds (optional)
$\frac{1}{8}$ tsp dried red pepper flakes

2 bay leaves or 4 curry leaves
50 ml (2 fl oz) vegetable oil
100 g (4 oz) desiccated (not sweetened or flaked) coconut
50 g (2 oz) finely chopped cashews

In a medium saucepan, bring the water and salt to the boil over medium-high heat. Stir in the rice, lower the heat, cover and simmer for 15 minutes or until tender and the water has been absorbed. While the rice is cooking, combine the mustard seeds, red pepper flakes, bay or curry leaves and vegetable oil in a large frying pan over medium-high heat.

Cook, stirring, until the mustard seeds begin to pop (1–2 minutes). Stir in the coconut and cashews and cook, stirring, until the coconut turns golden and the cashews turn light reddish brown. Stir the mixture into the cooked rice, taste for seasoning, remove the bay or curry leaves and serve.

Serves 4

variations

ancho–lime butter

see base recipe page 257

coriander butter
Prepare the basic recipe, using 50 g (2 oz) chopped fresh coriander and omitting the ground ancho.

fresh herb butter
Prepare the basic recipe, using 100 g (4 oz) chopped mixed fresh herbs such as basil, Italian parsley, marjoram and dill in place of coriander. Omit the ground ancho and lime juice. Season to taste with salt.

bistro butter
Prepare the basic recipe, using 50 g (2 oz) chopped mixed fresh herbs such as basil, Italian parsley, marjoram and dill in place of coriander. Omit the ground ancho and lime juice. Add 1 tablespoon chopped shallots. Season to taste with salt.

sun-dried tomato butter
Prepare the basic recipe, using 1 tablespoon finely chopped sun-dried tomato packed in oil in place of ground ancho.

herbed tomato vinaigrette

see base recipe page 258

chimichurri sauce
Prepare the basic recipe, omitting the tomatoes and decreasing the salt and pepper to ½ teaspoon each.

lemon-dill vinaigrette
Prepare the basic recipe, omitting the tomatoes and decreasing the salt and pepper to ½ teaspoon each. Use chopped fresh dill in place of the coriander, mint and oregano and fresh lemon juice in place of the sherry vinegar.

tarragon vinaigrette
Prepare the basic recipe, omitting the tomatoes and decreasing the salt and pepper to ½ teaspoon each. Use chopped fresh tarragon in place of the coriander, mint and oregano and tarragon vinegar in place of the sherry vinegar.

tarragon-orange vinaigrette
Prepare the basic recipe, omitting the tomatoes and decreasing the salt and pepper to ½ teaspoon each. Use chopped fresh tarragon in place of the coriander, mint and oregano and orange juice in place of the sherry vinegar. Add 1–2 teaspoons grated fresh orange zest.

variations

rémoulade

see base recipe page 261

creole rémoulade
Prepare the basic recipe, adding bottled hot sauce or Cajun seasoning to taste.

prawn rémoulade
Prepare the basic recipe. Combine 700 g (1½ lb) cooked prawns with the rémoulade and serve over baby greens.

crab cakes rémoulade
Prepare the basic recipe. Serve drizzled over Crab Cakes (page 105).

rosy rémoulade
Prepare the basic recipe, add 1 tablespoon tomato paste and stir to blend.

aïoli

see base recipe page 262

easy aïoli
Instead of the basic recipe, put 225 g (8 oz) mayonnaise in a bowl. Stir in 2 large garlic cloves, minced; 1 teaspoon fresh lemon juice; and salt and pepper, to taste.

easy rouille
Prepare the basic recipe, adding ¼ teaspoon saffron threads to the ingredients in the food processor, then process.

classic tartare sauce
Instead of the basic recipe, put 225 g (8 oz) mayonnaise in a bowl. Stir in 50 g (2 oz) dill pickle relish and season to taste.

sesame mayonnaise
Instead of the basic recipe, put 225 g (8 oz) mayonnaise in a bowl. Stir in 1½ teaspoons soya sauce and 1½ teaspoons toasted sesame oil.

variations

blender hollandaise

see base recipe page 264

browned butter hollandaise
Prepare the basic recipe, using butter that has been melted and then cooked until it starts to turn brown.

orange hollandaise
Prepare the basic recipe, adding 1 teaspoon freshly grated orange zest to the ingredients in the blender or food processor.

tarragon hollandaise
Prepare the basic recipe, adding 1 teaspoon dried tarragon and 1 teaspoon tarragon vinegar to the ingredients in the blender or food processor.

ancho-lime hollandaise
Prepare the basic recipe, adding 1 teaspoon freshly grated lime zest and 1 teaspoon ground ancho to the ingredients in the blender or food processor.

mango & lime salsa

see base recipe page 265

pineapple & lime salsa
Prepare the basic recipe, using chopped fresh pineapple in place of mango.

papaya & lime salsa
Prepare the basic recipe, using chopped fresh papaya in place of mango.

watermelon, jicama & lime salsa
Prepare the basic recipe, using 225 g (8 oz) deseeded and chopped
watermelon and 225 g (8 oz) grated jicama in place of mango.

honeydew & lime salsa
Prepare the basic recipe, using chopped honeydew melon in place of mango.
Add more fresh lime juice to taste.

variations

baja slaw

see base recipe page 266

courgette & fennel slaw
Prepare the basic recipe, using grated fresh courgette in place of red cabbage, thinly sliced fresh bulb fennel in place of green cabbage and 100 g (4 oz) mayonnaise in place of soured cream.

mustard slaw
Prepare the basic recipe, using 100 g (4 oz) mayonnaise in place of soured cream and 1 tablespoon Dijon mustard in place of lime and lemon juice.

sweet celery seed slaw
Prepare the basic recipe, using 100 ml (4 fl oz) vegetable oil in place of soured cream and 1 tablespoon celery seeds in place of lime and lemon juice. Add 2 tablespoons sugar to the dressing.

lemon-dill slaw
Prepare the basic recipe, using white wine vinegar in place of tarragon and lemon juice in place of lime juice. Add 1 teaspoon dried dill.

tomato–spinach orzo

see base recipe page 268

tomato–rocket orzo
Prepare the basic recipe, using 450 g (1 lb) baby rocket in place of spinach.

tomato–basil orzo
Prepare the basic recipe, using 225 g (8 oz) fresh basil leaves in place of
spinach and finely chopped fontina cheese in place of feta.

cucumber–dill orzo
Prepare the basic recipe, using 450 g (1 lb) chopped cucumber in place of
spinach and 225 g (8 oz) pitted, chopped Kalamata olives in place of
tomatoes. Add 2 teaspoons dried dill to the dressing.

butternut squash, sage & parmesan orzo
Prepare the basic recipe, omitting the tomatoes and spinach and using 450 g
(1 lb) cubed and cooked butternut squash. Use 225 g (8 oz) freshly grated
Parmesan in place of feta. Sauté 8 fresh sage leaves in olive oil until crisp
and stir into the Orzo just before serving.

variations

frites

see base recipe page 269

sweet potato fries
Prepare the basic recipe, using sweet potatoes in place of baking potatoes.

parsnip, carrot & potato fries
Prepare the basic recipe, using a mixture of parsnips, large carrots and baking potatoes in place of potatoes.

saratoga chips
Prepare the basic recipe, slicing the potatoes into ½-cm (¼-in) thin rounds instead of sticks.

potato, sweet potato & beet chips
Prepare the basic recipe, using a mixture of baking potatoes, sweet potatoes and large unpeeled beets in place of potatoes. Slice the vegetables into ½-cm (¼-in) thin rounds instead of sticks.

variations

coconut rice

see base recipe page 270

lemon rice
Prepare the basic recipe, adding 100 g (4 oz) chopped green onion,
50 g (2 oz) chopped fresh coriander and 25 g (1 oz) chopped green chilli
in place of the coconut. Fry until the vegetables are softened and cashews
are reddish brown. Stir the mixture into the rice along with 50 ml (2 fl oz)
fresh lemon juice.

saffron rice
Prepare the basic recipe, adding ½ teaspoon saffron threads to the rice as it
is cooking. Omit the coconut.

tex-mex rice
Cook the rice according to the basic recipe. Instead of all the other
ingredients, stir in 225 g (8 oz) chopped tinned tomato with green chillies,
undrained, 50 g (2 oz) chopped fresh coriander, 100 g (4 oz) crumbed queso
fresco and 1 tablespoon Ancho-Lime Butter (page 257). Season to taste.

coriander rice
Cook the rice according to the basic recipe. Instead of all the other
ingredients, stir in 225 g (8 oz) chopped fresh coriander and 2 tablespoons
fresh lime juice. Season to taste.

index